Pocket
AUSTIN

TOP SIGHTS • LOCAL LIFE • MADE EASY

Amy C Balfour

In This Book

QuickStart Guide

Your keys to understanding the city – we help you decide what to do and how to do it

Need to Know
Tips for a smooth trip

Neighborhoods
What's where

Explore Austin

The best things to see and do, neighborhood by neighborhood

Top Sights
Make the most of your visit

Local Life
The insider's city

The Best of Austin

The city's highlights in handy lists to help you plan

Best Walks
See the city on foot

Austin's Best...
The best experiences

Survival Guide

Tips and tricks for a seamless, hassle-free city experience

Getting Around
Travel like a local

Essential Information
Including where to stay

Our selection of the city's best places to eat, drink and experience:

◉ **Sights**

✖ **Eating**

🍷 **Drinking**

✦ **Entertainment**

🔒 **Shopping**

These symbols give you the vital information for each listing:

📞	Telephone Numbers	👪	Family-Friendly
🕙	Opening Hours	🐾	Pet-Friendly
🅿	Parking	🚌	Bus
🚭	Nonsmoking	⛴	Ferry
@	Internet Access	Ⓜ	Metro
🛜	Wi-Fi Access	Ⓢ	Subway
🥗	Vegetarian Selection	🚊	Tram
📖	English-Language Menu	🚆	Train

Find each listing quickly on maps for each neighborhood:

Bar Hemingway

16 🍷 Map p233, B2

Legend has it that Hemi self, wielding a machine rate this timber-pan ered bar during showpiece is a en by Papa ar town. Dress s.com; Hôtel Rit ; 🕙6.30pm-2a

Lonely Planet's Austin

Lonely Planet Pocket Guides are designed to get you straight to the heart of the city.

Inside you'll find all the must-see sights, plus tips to make your visit to each one really memorable. We've split the city into easy-to-navigate neighborhoods and provided clear maps so you'll find your way around with ease. Our expert authors have searched out the best of the city: walks, food, nightlife and shopping, to name a few. Because you want to explore, our 'Local Life' pages will take you to some of the most exciting areas to experience the real Austin.

And of course you'll find all the practical tips you need for a smooth trip: itineraries for short visits, how to get around, and how much to tip the guy who serves you a drink at the end of a long day's exploration.

It's your guarantee of a really great experience.

Our Promise

You can trust our travel information because Lonely Planet authors visit the places we write about, each and every edition. We never accept freebies for positive coverage, so you can rely on us to tell it like it is.

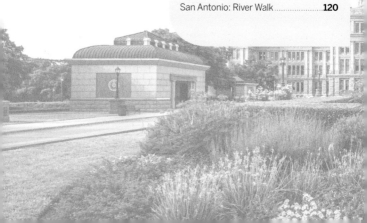

The Best of Austin 123

Austin's Best Walks

Austin's Best...

Survival Guide 141

QuickStart Guide

Welcome to Austin

A big city with a small-town heart, Austin earns the love with great music, fantastic parks, culinary prowess and an irresistible sociable streak. The South by Southwest (SXSW) and Austin City Limits music festivals enjoy international acclaim, but quality performances go down nightly. Parks thrum with hikers, runners and cyclists, who refuel at world-class food trucks. 'Hey ya'll' friendliness ties it all together.

Downtown Austin
MIKE HOLP/SHUTTERSTOCK ©

Austin
Top Sights

Texas State Capitol
(p26)

Big history, big building.

Bob Bullock Texas State History Museum (p28)

Remember the Alamo and more!

at Colony Under the Congress Avenue Bridge (p58)

atch the nightly swarm.

Zilker Park (p60)

Family fun on water and land.

Lyndon Baines Johnson (LBJ) Library & Museum (p82)

LBJ's story and accomplishments.

GEORGE WASHINGTON STATUE BY SCULPTOR POMPEO COPPINI

PNG STUDIO PHOTOGRAPHY/SHUTTERSTOCK ©

University of Texas (p84)

Become a Longhorn for a day.

Mount Bonnell (p106)

102 steps to big views.

ady Bird Johnson /ildflower Center (p62)

lowers, trees and views galore.

San Antonio: The Alamo (p118)

San Antonio's historic icon.

STEPHEN B. GOODWIN/SHUTTERSTOCK ©

San Antonio: River Walk (p120)

Riverfront pathway passing missions and parks.

Austin Local Life

*Local experiences and hidden gem
to help you uncover the real cit*

To really get a feel for the city and its denizens, spend your time wandering the side streets, sipping lattes in low-key coffee shops and sampling beer and tacos at longtime neighborhood favorites – the places you don't see in the glossy magazine profiles.

Downtown: Politics & Culture (p30)

☑ Historic buildings ☑ Cool cafes

ast Austin Nightlife (p44)

☑ Bar-hopping ☑ Neighborhood dining

Urban Hike: Zilker Park & Barton Creek Greenbelt (p78)

☑ Outdoor activities ☑ Family fun

South Congress Stroll (p64)

☑Indie shops ☑Superb people-watching

Dripping Springs Walking Tour: Small Town Exploring (p108)

☑Small-town charm ☑Dance hall nights

Other great places to experience the city like a local:

Market Stroll (p94)
☑ Book and music stores ☑ Graffiti walls

Austin
Day Planner

Day One

Start your day with gingerbread pancakes at **Kerbey Lane Cafe** (p99) then head to the **Bob Bullock Texas State History Museum** (p28), where the Austin City Limits exhibit – with its music videos of live performances – sets an upbeat mood for exploring. Once you've gotten your history fix, pop in to the **Blanton Museum of Art** (p29) across the street for eye-catching art.

Stroll Guadalupe St, aka the Drag, in search of lunch and swing by the **Hi, How Are You mural** (p88) and its smile from Jeremiah the Frog. In the afternoon, cool off at **Barton Springs Pool** (p79), where you can work up an appetite for Tex-Mex at **Trudy's Texas Star** (p88).

After dark, sit on the patio for dining and drinking at **Easy Tiger** (p37) and take your pick of sandwiches and craft beers. Next, plug into Austin's live-music scene with some club-hopping along Red River or in the Warehouse District.

Day Two

On day two, explore the **Texas State Capitol** (p30), starting inside with a free guided tour. Don't miss the towering dome over the rotunda.

Head to South Congress Ave for lunch at **Güero's Taco Bar** (p73), followed by boot shopping at **Allens Boots** (p65) and old-fashioned candy at **Big Top Candy Shop** (p65). Take a selfie beside the **I Love You So Much mural** (p68) then settle in at a table on a sidewalk patio for people-watching. Stroll around Lady Bird Lake on the **Ann & Roy Butler Hike-and-Bike Trail & Boardwalk** (p68).

If it's summer, make your way towards the Congress Avenue Bridge to witness the nightly exodus of America's largest urban **bat colony** (p58). End your evening with Texas two-stepping at the **Broken Spoke** (p74). If you're a little worried about your style, it offers lessons nightly Wednesday through Saturday.

Short on time?
We've arranged Austin's must-sees into these day-by-day itineraries to make sure you see the very best of the city in the time you have available.

Day Three

☀ On day three, it's time for a road trip to Dripping Springs, known as the Gateway to the Hill Country. This rural community is 25 miles west of Austin. In the morning jump into the refreshing swimming hole at **Hamilton Pool Preserve** (p112), which is tucked in a green wonderland. Reservations are often required so check before you leave.

☀ From here, grab lunch at one of two acclaimed restaurants: barbecue at **Salt Lick** (p113) or pizza at **Pieous** (p113). Spend the afternoon visiting wineries, microbreweries and distilleries, followed by a stroll though the historic downtown and a cup off coffee at **Mazama Coffee Co** (p108).

☾ In the evening, forget your calorie counting with gourmet Southern comfort food at **Homespun** (p109). Enjoy an after-dinner beer at the **Barber Shop** (p109). On Thursday, Friday and Saturday nights walk over to the **Mercer Street Dance Hall** (p109) where live music, cold beer and lively dancing are always a blast.

Day Four

☀ The next day, check out a couple of the smaller museums around town. Downtown, you can see creative works from Mexican and Mexican American artists, oddities from around the globe, and contemporary art. On the campus of the University of Texas, you'll find the impressive bones of a Cretaceous-era flying reptile at the **Texas Memorial Museum** (p88) and loads of personal and political information about President Lyndon B Johnson at the **Lyndon Baines Johnson (LBJ) Library & Museum** (p82). A rare Gutenberg bible is displayed at **Harry Ransom Humanities Research Center** (p85).

☀ For lunch, hit up one of the city's many barbecue joints. In the afternoon, enjoy some outdoor time by hiking up to the summit of **Mount Bonnell** (p106), or strolling through the flowers and plant life at the **Lady Bird Johnson Wildflower Center** (p62).

☾ Make dinner a moveable feast by roaming the food trucks. End with a live show at the **Continental Club** (p74) on South Congress Avenue.

Need to Know

**For more information,
see Survival Guide (p141)**

Currency
US dollar ($)

Language
English

Visas
Visas are not required for citizens of Visa Waiver Program (VWP) countries, but you must request travel authorization from ESTA at least 72 hours in advance. Visitors not eligible for the program will require a B-2 tourism visa in advance of their arrival.

Money
ATMs are widely available. Credit cards are widely accepted and are generally required for advance hotel reservations and car rentals.

Mobile Phones
Local prepaid SIM cards are widely available, though network reception can be spotty in rural areas. Only foreign phones that operate on tri- or quad-band frequencies will work in the USA.

Time
Central Time Zone (GMT/UTC minus five hours).

Plugs & Adaptors
120V/60Hz

Tipping
Tipping is not optional. Service employees make minimum wage and rely on tips.

❶ Before You Go

Your Daily Budget

Budget: Less than $120
► Campground or dorm bed: $10–40
► Basic motel room: $60–95
► Tacos, pizza or take-out: $2–15
► Bus: $3.50

Midrange: $200–300
► B&B or better quality motel: $120–195
► Cafe meals & food-truck takeout: $6–25
► Compact car rental & fuel: $50
► Movies, museums & admissions: $15

Top End: More than $350
► Upscale hotel: $300–655
► Restaurant meals & fine dining: from $30
► Intermediate to luxury car rental & fuel: $50–95
► Museums, shows, major attractions, theme parks: $30–55

Useful Websites

Austin Chronicle (www.austinchronicle.com) Alternative weekly newspaper with music, arts, restaurant and outdoor guides.

Austin Insider Guide (www.austintexas.org) Official city tourism website.

Austin360 (www.austin360.com) American-Statesman's encyclopedic city guide.

Advance Planning

Plan well ahead for South by Southwest (SXSW). The most affordable option is to buy early-bird tickets before mid-September. The price increases approximately $100 per month after that until showtime. Hotel rooms fill months ahead of time.

② Arriving in Austin

✈ From Austin-Bergstrom International Airport

About 10 miles southeast of downtown, the airport is served by Air Canada, Alaska Airlines, Allegiant, American, British Airways, Delta, Frontier, JetBlue, Southwest and United.

Transportation Options

► Ground transportation leaves from the lower level near baggage claim.

► A taxi between the airport and downtown costs $25 to $30.

► Capital Metro (CapMetro; Map p32; ☏512-474-1200, transit store 512-389-7454; www.capmetro.org; transit store 209 W 9th St; ⏱transit store 7:30am-5:30pm Mon-Fri) runs a limited-stop Airport Flyer (bus 100) service between the airport and downtown and the University of Texas for $1.25 each way, with departures every 30 minutes. It takes at least 20 minutes to get downtown from the airport, and 35 minutes to reach the UT campus.

► SuperShuttle (☏800-258-3826; www.supershuttle.com) offers a shared-van service from the airport to downtown hotels for about $14 one way, or a few dollars more to accommodations along N I-35 and near the Arboretum Mall.

► You can walk from the terminal to the rental car facility. All major rental car agencies are represented.

③ Getting Around

You can explore several communities by foot: downtown, the Market District, S Congress Ave in South Austin, E 6th St in East Austin and the University of Texas. You will need to drive or catch a bus between most of these neighborhoods, however. You can also walk to Lady Bird Lake from downtown and S Congress Ave.

🚗 Car & Motorcycle

If you plan to explore several neighborhoods, consider renting a car. You will also need wheels for day trips to Dripping Springs and Lockhart. You will have to pay a meter for street parking downtown or a small fee at a garage. Elsewhere parking is free but check signage for permit and time limit requirements.

🚌 Bus

Capital Metro runs the public-transit system. Call for directions to anywhere or step into the downtown Capital Metro Transit Store for information. Regular city buses – not the more expensive express routes – cost $1.25. Children under six are free. There are bicycle racks on the front of almost all CapMetro buses, including more than a dozen UT shuttle routes.

🚲 Bicycle

The city offers bike-sharing, with more than 40 Austin B-cycle (www.austin.bcycle.com) stations in the city.

🚗 Rideshare & Taxi

For ride sharing, try Fare (www.ridefare.com), Fasten (www.fasten.com) or the non-profit Ride Austin (www.rideaustin.com). Uber (www.uber.com) and Lyft (www.lyft.com) recently returned to Austin. For a cab, you'll usually need to call and request one, rather than flagging one on the street.

Austin Neighborhoods

Mt Bonnell

West Austin (p104)
Drive west for views and jaunts into nature, followed by easy conviviality at microbreweries, distilleries and wineries.

◉ Top Sights
Mount Bonnell

Market District, Clarksville & North Austin (p92)
Close to downtown, the Market District and Clarksville are made for strolling and shopping. North Austin has good dinner options.

Zilker Park

South Austin (p56)
Eclectic shops and eateries line S Congress Ave; fun beckons at Zilker Park.

◉ Top Sights
Bat Colony Under the Congress Ave Bridge

Zilker Park

Lady Bird Johnson Wildflower Center

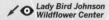
Lady Bird Johnson Wildflower Center

San Antonio (73mi)

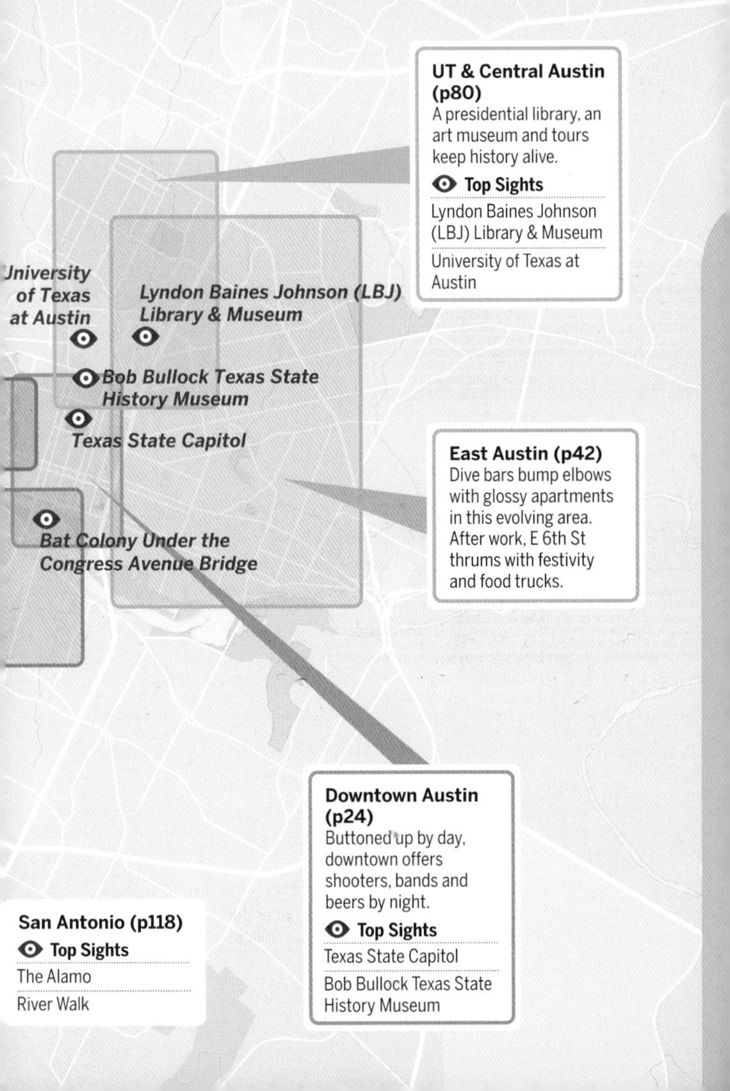

UT & Central Austin (p80)
A presidential library, an art museum and tours keep history alive.

⊙ Top Sights

Lyndon Baines Johnson (LBJ) Library & Museum

University of Texas at Austin

University of Texas at Austin ⊙

Lyndon Baines Johnson (LBJ) Library & Museum ⊙

⊙ Bob Bullock Texas State History Museum

⊙ Texas State Capitol

⊙ Bat Colony Under the Congress Avenue Bridge

East Austin (p42)
Dive bars bump elbows with glossy apartments in this evolving area. After work, E 6th St thrums with festivity and food trucks.

Downtown Austin (p24)
Buttoned up by day, downtown offers shooters, bands and beers by night.

⊙ Top Sights

Texas State Capitol

Bob Bullock Texas State History Museum

San Antonio (p118)

⊙ Top Sights

The Alamo

River Walk

Explore
Austin

Worth a Trip

Congress Avenue Bridge (p58) with Texas
State Capitol (p26) in background
TOD GRUBBS/BEECREEKPHOTOGRAPHY/500PX ©

Explore

Downtown Austin

Downtown is the hardworking hub of the city, home to the state capitol complex, several museums and numerous hotels catering to politicians, business travelers and convention-goers. Downtown plays hard, too. The neighborhood is chock-full of entertainment options, including the wild shot bars of 6th St, the more low-key bars of Rainey St and music venues in Red River.

The Sights in a Day

Begin at the **state capitol** (p26). You can join a guided tour or pick up a self-guided tour pamphlet. Don't miss the rotunda – look up, down and around for the full effect. Statues dot the pretty lawn and you'll find a small museum in the freestanding **Capitol Visitors Center** (p147).

After lunch at **Coopers Old Time Pit Bar-B-Cue** (p36) – try the jalapeño mac-and-cheese – take your pick of three great museums. Displays are offbeat at the **Museum of the Weird** (p34), while the up-to-the-minute exhibits by Mexican artists at the wonderful **Mexic-Arte Museum** (p31) are always intriguing. Works are similarly compelling at the **Contemporary Austin** (p34).

In warmer months, walk to Lady Bird Lake just before sunset to view the nightly migration of Mexican free-tailed **bats** (p58) from beneath the Congress Avenue Bridge. In colder months, enjoy a drink at the **Driskill Hotel** (p31) bar followed by dinner at **Easy Tiger** (p37). Then enjoy a band at **Stubb's Bar-B-Q** (p38) and wander the bars on Rainey St.

For a local's day downtown, see p30.

👁 Top Sights

Texas State Capitol (p26)

Bob Bullock Texas State History Museum (p28)

🔍 Local Life

Downtown: Politics & Culture (p30)

❤ Best of Austin

Eating

Lamberts (p36)

Moonshine Patio Bar & Grill (p36)

Drinking & Nightlife

Easy Tiger (p37)

Stubb's Bar-B-Q (p38)

Getting There

🚌 **Bus** Capital Metro (p145) routes between 1 and 99 connect with downtown. The 100 Airport Flyer runs between downtown and the airport.

🚗 **Car** The north–south MoPac Expy/Hwy Loop 1 borders downtown to the west. I-35 parallels MoPac to the east.

🚆 **Train** The Texas Eagle stops at the Amtrak station just west of downtown.

Top Sights
Texas State Capitol

Built in 1888 from sunset-red granite, this state capitol is the largest in the US, backing up the ubiquitous claim that everything is bigger in Texas. If nothing else, take a peek at the lovely rotunda – be sure to look up at the dome – and try out the whispering gallery created by its curved ceiling.

👁 Map p32, D3

📞512-463-5495, tours 512-463-0063

cnr 11th St & Congress Ave

admission free

🕐7am-10pm Mon-Fri, 9am-8pm Sat & Sun

♿

South Foyer

Loaded with sculptures and artwork, the South Foyer is an inspiring place to begin your trip through the capitol building. It's also the starting point for guided tours. Statues of local heroes Stephen F Austin and Sam Houston stand nobly beside the entrance to the rotunda. Alamo fighter Davy Crockett is honored in a grand painting by Texas artist William Henry Huddle. Crockett's portrait adorns the wall across from an equally grand painting of the *Surrender of Santa Anna*, also painted by Huddle. African American politicians serving the state prior to 1900 are shown in a composite beside the rotunda.

The Rotunda & Dome

It's hard to know which way to look when entering the massive rotunda on the first level. There's an eye-catching feature in every direction. On the floor, the seals of the six countries whose flags have flown over Texas surround the Great Seal. Six?! Yep. Spain, France, Mexico, the Republic of Texas (a country from 1836-1845), the Confederate States of America and the US. The star in the dome overhead is 218 feet above you and the seemingly tiny star actually stretches 8ft across.

Legislative Chambers

Texas history comes to life in two massive paintings on the back wall of the Senate chamber: the clash at the Alamo and the battle of San Jacinto. Thirty-one state senators meet in this 2nd-storey chamber. The 150 members of the House of Representatives meet across the rotunda in a separate chamber. To see the government in action, take a seat in the 3rd-floor visitor balconies overlooking the House of Representatives and Senate chamber galleries, which are open to the public when the state legislature is in session (odd-numbered years from mid January through May or June).

☑ **Top Tips**

▶ Free two-hour parking is available inside the Capitol Visitors Parking Garage (p144), entered from either 12th St or 13th St, off San Jacinto Blvd.

▶ You'll find an exhibit about the capitol building in the free-standing visitor center on the southeast corner of the grounds.

▶ Self-guided-tour brochures of the capitol building and grounds are available inside the tour guide office on the ground floor. From here you can also take one of the interesting 40-minute guided tours offered daily. The green sprawl of the capitol grounds and its monuments are worth a stroll before or after your tour.

✖ **Take a Break**

Enjoy lunch at longtime favorite the Texas Chili Parlor (p35).

For a caffeine pick-me-up, walk south to Hideout Coffee House & Theatre (p31).

Top Sights
Bob Bullock
Texas State History Museum

This is no dusty historical museum. Big and glitzy, it shows off the Lone Star State's history, from when it used to be part of Mexico up to the present, with high-tech interactive exhibits and fun theatrics.

👁 Map p32, D1

📞 512-936-8746

www.thestoryoftexas.com

1800 Congress Ave

adult/child $13/9

🕐 9am-5pm Mon-Sat, noon-5pm Sun

La Belle: The Ship That Changed History

A new permanent exhibit on the 1st floor showcases the history – and the recovered hull – of *La Belle*, a French ship that sank off the Gulf Coast in the 1680s, changing the course of Texas history. Exhibits explore the ship's remarkable story: sent by King Louis XIV of France under the command of René-Robert Cavelier, Sieur de la Salle, *La Belle* was one of four vessels carrying 400 passengers to the new world, where they were to establish a colony and trade routes. All four ships were eventually lost, with *La Belle* sinking off the Texas coast in 1686. Archaeologists have recovered 1.4 million artifacts; muskets, glass beads and farming tools are currently on display.

Story of Texas

The Texas History galleries are the core of the museum, and more than 700 artifacts are displayed. The 1st floor focuses on *La Belle*, while exhibits on the 2nd floor trace Texas history from 1821 to 1936. A statue of Texas statesman and hero Sam Houston marks the entrance. As you explore, you'll discover more about Texas booster Stephen F Austin (check out his pine desk) and learn more about the Alamo, Texas Comanches and the lives of African Americans. Oil and cattle exhibits are highlights on the 3rd floor while the Austin City Limits display livens up the scene with music.

IMAX & the Star of Destiny

The museum also houses Austin's first IMAX theater (check website for listings; adult/child 4-17yr $9/7) and the Texas Spirit Theater (adult/child 4-17yr $5/4). Both offer discounted combination tickets when bought with a museum admission. The Texas Spirit Theater is where you can see *The Star of Destiny*, a 15-minute special-effects film that's simultaneously high-tech and hokey fun.

☑ Top Tips

▶ Don't waste too much time driving around looking for parking. The lot beneath the building is convenient and costs a flat $8.

▶ The always compelling Blanton Museum of Art (p85) is across the street, so save an extra hour to check it out.

✗ Take a Break

If all that history has you craving Tex-Mex and a margarita, don't worry, Trudy's Texas Star (p88) has you covered. You could also grab a beer at Scholz Garten (p90).

Q Local Life
Downtown: Politics & Culture

Downtown is a lively jumble of politicians, office workers, tourists, creatives and a fair number of homeless folks. Cops on bikes patrol the area, particularly near gritty 6th St, but generally the streets are safe. Lined with historic buildings, art museums and cool cafes, Congress Ave is the main thoroughfare, and it's an invigorating place to stroll.

1 Capitol Grounds
Crowds can be distracting in the **state capitol building** (p26), but the sprawling grounds are typically tranquil. Here, an easy, tree-lined walk passes 20 statues and memorials. On the south lawn look for the Texas cowboy and a monument honoring heroes of the Alamo. The Tejano Monument spotlights the contributions of Spanish and Mexican settlers to the state's history and culture.

❷ Congress Avenue

Austin was established in 1839 to serve as the capital of the Republic of Texas. Development plans called for a 120-foot wide ceremonial boulevard stretching from the capitol to the Colorado River. No buildings from that era survive, but the grand boulevard – Congress Ave – still thrives. Today, buildings date from various eras. The **Paramount Theatre** (p40) celebrated its 100th anniversary in 2015.

❸ Caffeine Fix

Scruffy and crowded, **Hideout Coffee House** (p38) stands apart from the competition because of the small improv theater in the back. Step in for a latte, a pastry and maybe some audience participation.

❹ Driskill Bar

This **clubby place** (p40) feels like Texas. There's a longhorn steer mounted over the fireplace, a copper tin ceiling overhead and cowhide covers on the chairs. And lots of private areas to loosen your tie or kick off your heels. Join politicians, screenwriters, musicians and everyone else in search of a good cocktail in a bar that knows what it's doing.

❺ Movie Lovers Unite

Cinephiles flock to **Alamo Drafthouse** (p38) for food, beer and a great movie-going experience. Think comfy seats and absolutely no tolerance for talking or cell phone use. An Austin original, Alamo Drafthouses are now scattered across the state and venturing into non-Texas territory. Check the online calendar (the Ritz location) for dance parties, Girlie Night (watch *The Notebook*!) and Terror Tuesday flicks.

❻ Mexic-Arte Museum

The exhibits rotate regularly at this airy contemporary **museum** (p34), so popping in always feels like a mini-adventure. Even better, it's a small place, so you can immerse in the art – which spotlights Mexican and Latino works – and never feel rushed. If you're looking for a unique present, the gift shop is loaded with eclectic arts and crafts.

E 8th St
E 6th St
E 5th St
E 4th St
E 3rd St
E 2nd St
Willow St
Spence St
Brushy St
San Marcos St

18

Interregional Hwy

E 8th St
E 7th St
N IH 35 Frontage Rd
12

Sabine St

Neches St

Museum of
the Weird

3

Austin Visitor
Information
Center

Palm
Park

290
35

S IH 35 Frontage Rd

Red River St

11

24
15
22

E 5th St

9

Driskill St

Brush
Park

Davis St

River St

Rainey St

13

20

E 7th St

Downtown

Trinity St

Austin
Convention
Center

Red River St

17

E 6th St

Brazos St

19

E 4th St

E 3rd St

E 2nd St

E Cesar Chavez St (E 1st St)

W 6th St

14

Colorado St

DOWNTOWN

Mexic-Arte
Museum

1

25

Congress Ave

7

23

W 4th St

16

Colorado St

W 3rd St

W 2nd St

Congress Ave
Bridge

Republic
Square

W 5th St

Guadalupe St

San Antonio St

5

Mellow
Johnny's
Bike Shop

8

27

WAREHOUSE
DISTRICT

10

W Cesar Chavez St (W 1st St)

1st St S

Lady Bird Lake

Shoal
Creek
Greenbelt

Ann & Roy Butler
Hike & Bike
Trail & Boardwalk

Vic Mathias
Shores

500 m
0.25 miles

For reviews see

◉	Top Sights	p26
◉	Sights	p34
✕	Eating	p35
🍷	Drinking	p37
✿	Entertainment	p38
🛍	Shopping	p41

Sights

Mexic-Arte Museum　　MUSEUM

1 Map p32, C5

This wonderful, eclectic downtown museum features works from Mexican and Mexican American artists in exhibitions that rotate every two months. The museum's holdings include carved wooden masks, modern Latin American paintings, historic photographs and contemporary art. Don't miss the back gallery, where new and experimental talent is shown. Admission is free on Sundays. (☏512-480-9373; www.mexic-artemuseum.org; 419 Congress Ave; adult/child under 12yr/student $5/1/4; ☺10am-6pm Mon-Thu, to 5pm Fri & Sat, noon-5pm Sun)

Historic Walking Tours　　WALKING

2 Map p32, C3

One of the best deals around are the free Historic Walking Tours of downtown Austin, which leave from the capitol's south steps. Tours last between 60 and 90 minutes. Make reservations at least 48 hours in advance either online or by phone through the visitor center. (☏512-474-5171; www.tspb.state.tx.us/plan/tours/tours.html; admission free; ☺9am Tue & Thu-Sat, 11am & 1pm Sun)

Museum of the Weird　　MUSEUM

3 Map p32, D5

Pay the entrance fee, walk through the gift shop and then step inside Austin's version of a cabinet of curiosities. Or perhaps we should say hallway of curiosities, one lined with shrunken heads, malformed mammals and a range of unusual artifacts. The show stealer? The legendary Minnesota Ice Man – is that a frozen prehistoric man under all that ice? Step up to see for yourself then grab a seat for a live show of amazing physical derring-do. (☏512-476-5493; www.museumoftheweird.com; 412 E 6th St; adult/child $12/8; ☺10am-midnight)

Contemporary Austin: Jones Center　　MUSEUM

4 Map p32, C4

This two-site museum has a new name and a freshly renovated downtown space. Downtown, the Jones Center features rotating exhibits representing new voices. Don't miss the view of the city from the new Moody Rooftop, an open-air event space. You'll also find temporary exhibits at the museum's

Til death do us part, by artist Federico Archuleta, fe-de-rico.com, Mexic-Arte Museum

original home at Laguna Gloria (p115). (☎512-453-5312; www.thecontemporaryaustin. org; 700 Congress Ave; adult/child under 18yr $5/free; ⏰11am-7pm Tue-Sat, noon-5pm Sun)

Mellow Johnny's
Bike Shop CYCLING

5 Map p32, A5

Say what you will about Lance Armstrong, you can still count on him to find you a pretty good bike. Located right downtown, Mellow Johnny's is co-owned by the disgraced seven-time Tour de France winner. It rents high-performance bikes as well as commuter bikes, and offers free guided bike rides (check the website for a schedule). (☎512-473-0222; www.

mellowjohnnys.com; 400 Nueces St; day use $20-50; ⏰7am-7pm Mon-Fri, 7am-6pm Sat, 8am-5pm Sun)

Eating

Texas Chili Parlor TEX-MEX $

6 Map p32, C2

Ready for an X-rated meal? When ordering your chili, keep in mind that 'X' is mild, 'XX' is spicy and 'XXX' is melt-your-face-off hot at this Austin institution. There's more than just chili on the menu; there's also Frito pie, which is chili over Fritos. Still not feeling it? There's also burgers, enchiladas and, of course, more chili.

(512-472-2828; 1409 Lavaca St; chili $4-9, mains $5-15; 11am-2am)

Coopers Old Time Pit Bar-B-Cue
BARBECUE $$

7 Map p32, C6

The downtown lunch crowd has discovered this new outpost of beloved Cooper's Bar-B-Cue in Llano. Pick your meat at the counter (paid by the pound) then add sides. We're partial to the jalapeño mac-and-cheese, which you won't want to share. The baked beans and the white bread are always free. (512-474-2145; www.coopersbbqaustin.com; 217 Congress Ave; beef ribs & brisket per lb $18, other meats vary; 11am-10pm)

La Condesa
MEXICAN $$

8 Map p32, B6

Here in slacky Slackerville, decor is often an afterthought, but La Condesa came along and changed all that with an eye-poppingly gorgeous space

Top Tip
Orientation
Downtown Austin is an orderly grid. The main north–south artery is Congress Ave, with Cesar Chavez St running east–west. Most downtown streets are one way, including 6th St, a major southbound thoroughfare, and southbound Guadalupe St (pronounced *guad*-ah-loop locally, despite what you might have learned in Spanish class).

that's colorful, supermodern and artsy, with a dazzling mural taking up an entire wall. If you find the dinners to be a little spendy, come for brunch (in the $9 to $20 range). (512-499-0300; www.lacondesa.com; 400 W 2nd St; lunch $11-14, dinner $10-25; 11:30am-2:30pm Mon-Fri, 11am-3pm Sat & Sun, 5-10pm Sun-Wed, to 11pm Thu-Sat)

Moonshine Patio Bar & Grill
AMERICAN $$

9 Map p32, D6

Dating from the mid-1850s, this historic building is a remarkably well preserved homage to Austin's early days. Within its exposed limestone walls, you can enjoy upscale comfort food, half-price appetizers at happy hour or a lavish Sunday brunch buffet ($20). Or chill on the patio under the shade of pecan trees. (512-236-9599; www.moonshinegrill.com; 303 Red River St; dinner mains $12-25; 11am-10pm Mon-Thu, to 11pm Fri & Sat, 9am-2pm & 5-10pm Sun)

Lamberts
BARBECUE $$$

10 Map p32, A6

Torn between barbecue and fine dining? Lambert's serves intelligent updates of American comfort-food classics – some might call it 'uppity barbecue' – in a historic stone building run by Austin chef Lou Lambert. (512-494-1500; www.lambertsaustin.com; 401 W 2nd St; lunch $12-19, dinner $19-42; 11am-2:30pm Mon-Sat, to 2pm Sun, 5:30-10pm Sun-Wed, to 10:30pm Thu-Sat)

Beware of the Goddess

She stood atop the Texas State Capitol for nearly 100 years, a star in one hand, a sword in the other. When the **Goddess of Liberty** was removed from her perch and lowered by helicopter as part of a capitol restoration project in 1985, no one had seen her up close since 1888. And, well, *wow*. How to put this? She was not a handsome woman.

Not only was she badly weathered, she was drop-dead ugly, with hideously exaggerated features meant to be appreciated from 300ft below. She was also 16ft tall. After making a cast for her replacement, they restored her to her former, er, beauty and dropped her off here as a display, meaning you can have a face-to-face with the woman people for decades could only admire from afar.

Chez Nous   FRENCH $$$

 11 · Map p32, D5

This classic Parisian-style bistro has been quietly serving excellent food since 1982. Low-key and casual, Chez Nous is as unpretentious as they come, and has made many a French food lover *trés heureux*, especially with its three-course *menu du jour* for $32.50. (☏512-473-2413; www.cheznousaustin.com; 510 Neches St; lunch $8-19, dinner mains $20-37; ⊘11:45am-2pm Tue-Fri, 6-10:30pm Tue-Sun)

Drinking

Easy Tiger   BEER GARDEN

 12 · Map p32, E6

The one bar on Dirty 6th that all locals love? Easy Tiger, an inside-outside beer garden overlooking Waller Creek. The place welcomes all comers with an upbeat communal vibe. Craft beers are listed on the chalkboard. And the artisanal sandwiches? Baked on tasty bread from the All bakery upstairs (7am to 2am). The meat is cooked in-house. (www.easytigeraustin.com; 709 E 6th St; ⊘11am-2am)

Craft Pride   BAR

 13 · Map p32, D8

If it ain't brewed in Texas, then it ain't on tap at this dark and cozy bar, which bursts with Lone Star pride. Yep, from the All Call kolsch to the Yellow Rose IPA, all 54 craft beers served here are produced in Texas. Look for the bar at the southern end of Rainey St. (☏512-428-5571; www.craftprideaustin.com; 61 Rainey St; ⊘4pm-2am Mon-Fri, 1pm-2am Sat, 1pm-1am Sun)

Garage   LOUNGE

 14 · Map p32, C5

Hidden inside a parking garage, this cozy, dimly lit lounge draws a hip but not overly precious Austin crowd who give high marks to the first-rate cocktails, handsomely designed space and novel location. (☎512-369-3490; www.garagetx.com; 503 Colorado St; ⏱5pm-2am Mon-Sat)

Casino El Camino

BAR

15 Map p32, D5

With a legendary jukebox and even better burgers, this is the spot for serious drinking and late-night carousing. If it's too dark inside, head for the back patio. (☎512-469-9330; 517 E 6th St; ⏱11:30am-2am)

Oilcan Harry's

CLUB

16 Map p32, B5

Oh, yes, there's dancing. And oh, yes, it's packed. (And how are you supposed to dance with all those people in there?) As much as the girls wish it were a mixed crowd, this scene is all about the boys. Sweaty ones. (☎512-320-8823; 211 W 4th St; ⏱2pm-2am Mon-Fri, noon-2am Sat & Sun)

Hideout Coffee House & Theatre

COFFEE

17 Map p32, C5

Despite its downtown location, it has a near-campus vibe and damn fine brews. (☎512-476-1313; 617 Congress Ave; ⏱7am-10pm Mon-Wed, to midnight Thu & Fri, 8am-noon Sat, 8am-10pm Sun; 🛜)

Entertainment

Stubb's Bar-B-Q

LIVE MUSIC

18 Map p32, E5

Stubb's has live music almost every night, with a great mix of premier local and touring acts from across the musical spectrum. Many warm-weather shows are held out back along Waller Creek. There are two stages, a smaller stage indoors and a larger backyard venue. (☎512-480-8341; www.stubbsaustin.com; 801 Red River St; ⏱11am-10pm Mon-Thu, to 11pm Fri & Sat, 10:30am-9pm Sun)

Antone's

LIVE MUSIC

19 Map p32, C5

A key player in Austin's musical history, Antone's has attracted the best of the blues and other popular local acts since 1975. All ages, all the time. (www.facebook.com/antonesnightclub; 305 E 5th St; ⏱showtimes vary)

Alamo Drafthouse Cinema

CINEMA

20 Map p32, D5

Easily the most fun you can have at the movies: sing along with *Grease,* quote along with *Princess Bride,* or just enjoy food and drink delivered right to your seat during first-run films. Check the website for other locations. (☎512-861-7020; www.drafthouse.com; 320 E 6th St; tickets $12-13)

Understand

History of Austin

Early Days

Things happened quickly in the early days of Austin. In 1837 – just one year after Texas had won its independence from Mexico – settlers founded the town of Waterloo on the banks of the Colorado River. By 1939 the town had been chosen as the state capital and renamed Austin, after Stephen F Austin, a man who had colonized the area and come to be known as the Father of Texas.

Damming the River

In 1960, the Colorado River was dammed near Austin, creating a lake known as Town Lake. Mayor Roy Johnson and Lady Bird Johnson, wife of former president Lyndon B Johnson, spearheaded efforts to improve the banks of the reservoir, leading the successful charge for new trails and landscaping. The lake was renamed in her honor in 2007.

After improvements in 1980, the Congress Avenue Bridge drew the attention of a colony of 1.5 million Mexican free-tailed bats, who now wow crowds with their nightly feeding migration.

Tech Boom

Fast forward to the 1990s, when the tech industry brought another boom. With a well-educated populace (thanks to all those University of Texas grads who never could quite bear to move away), Austin attracted major tech companies. It wasn't all UT grads fueling the movement: Michael Dell founded his computer company in his dorm room in 1984 and promptly dropped out of UT.

Between tech types, UT students, musicians and politicians, Austin has a near-constant influx of new residents. Things are constantly changing in the capital city, for better or for worse.

Local Life

Bar-Hopping Through History

Two of the city's most interesting bars are tucked inside top-notch lodging options that sit across the street from each other downtown. The Firehouse Lounge inhabits the **Firehouse Hostel** (📞512-201-2522; www.firehousehostel.com; 605 Brazos St;), which is the city's oldest freestanding fire station, with a facade built in 1885. Enter through the bookcase. The Driskill Hotel Bar is a clubby place with wall-mounted longhorns. It's nestled deep inside the **Driskill Hotel** (📞512-439-1234; www.driskillhotel.com; 604 Brazos St;), built by a cattle baron in the late 1800s.

Paramount Theatre   THEATER

21 ⭐ Map p32, C4

Dating from 1915, this old vaudevillian house has staged everything from splashy Broadway shows to stand-up comics to classic film screenings. (📞512-474-1221; www.austintheatre.org; 713 Congress Ave; ⊙box office noon-5:30pm Mon-Fri, 2hr before showtime Sat & Sun)

Esther's Follies   COMEDY

22 ⭐ Map p32, D5

Drawing from current events and pop culture, this long-running satire show has a vaudevillian slant, thanks to musical numbers and, yep, even a magician. Good, harmless fun. (📞512-320-0553; www.esthersfollies.com; 525 E 6th

St; reserved seating/general admission $30/25; ⊙shows 8pm Thu-Sat, plus 10pm Fri & Sat)

Cedar Street Courtyard   LIVE MUSIC

23 ⭐ Map p32, B5

Forget the dark and crowded club scene; this sophisticated courtyard venue serves martinis along with jazz and swing. (📞512-495-9669; www.cedarstreetaustin.com; 208 W 4th St; ⊙4pm-2am Mon-Fri, from 6pm Sat & Sun)

Flamingo Cantina   LIVE MUSIC

24 ⭐ Map p32, D5

Called 'the last place with soul on 6th,' Austin's premier reggae joint prides itself on its good rasta vibes and bouncy dance floor. Seat yourself on the carpeted bleachers for good views of the stage. (📞512-494-9336; www.flamingocantina.com; 515 E 6th St)

Elephant Room   LIVE MUSIC

25 ⭐ Map p32, C6

This intimate, subterranean jazz club has a cool vibe, and live music almost every night. The cover charge stays low, mostly free concerts on weekends, and there are happy-hour shows at 6pm weekdays. (📞512-473-2279; www.elephantroom.com; 315 Congress Ave; ⊙4pm-2am Mon-Fri, from 8pm Sat & Sun)

Hideout Coffee House & Theatre   COMEDY

The hipsters' Hideout (see 17 🔵 Map p32, C5) is a small coffeehouse–theater space that rubs shoulders with the big theaters on Congress Ave. Shows

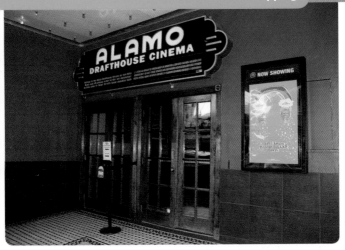

Alamo Drafthouse Cinema (p38)

here feature live improv with plenty of audience participation. The box office usually opens half an hour before showtime. (512-443-3688; www. hideouttheatre.com; 617 Congress Ave; tickets $5-15; ⊙ shows usually Thu-Sun)

Austin Symphony   PERFORMING ARTS

26 ⭐ Map p32, E4

Founded in the early 20th century, the city's oldest performing-arts group plays classical and pop music at numerous venues throughout the city. The main performance season runs from September to April. (512-476-6064; www.austinsymphony.org; box office

1101 Red River St; tickets $12-55; ⊙ box office 9am-5pm Mon-Thu, to 4pm Fri, noon-5pm Sat performance days only, 2hr before showtime performance days)

Shopping

Toy Joy   TOYS

27 🛍 Map p32, A6

This colorful toy store for grown-ups and big kids is an exuberant repository that's packed floor to ceiling with fun. (512-320-0090; www.toyjoy.com; 403 W 2nd St; ⊙ 10am-9pm)

Explore

East Austin

East Austin is on the rise. Just look at all the construction cranes along gentrifying E 6th St. Old-timers will warn you that east of I-35 is dangerous and to be avoided at night. Although the streets retain a gritty feel, and host their fair share of vagrants, the main thoroughfares feel safe. The neighborhood also has a rich history as an African American community, with roots back to the 19th century.

The Sights in a Day

☀ If you're in the mood for exercise, enjoy a morning stroll on the eastern fringes of the **hike-and-bike trail** (p68) looping around Lady Bird Lake. Another option is an hour or two of indoor rock climbing at the **Austin Bouldering Project** (p48). Kids will enjoy the hands-on science and art projects at the **Thinkery** (p48).

☀ Sample the food truck offerings by ordering tacos at **Veracruz All Natural** (p49) or the sandwiches at **Paperboy** (p51). Learn about regional African-American history at the **George Washington Carver Museum** (p48) then look for the grave of city namesake Stephen F Austin at the **Texas State Cemetery** (pictured left; p48). For a coffee break, and maybe some bicycle talk, pop into **Flat Track Coffee** (p54).

☾ Gussy up – just a tiny bit – for an oh-so-tasty dinner of farm-fresh fare at **Dai Due** (p52) or modern down-home cooking at the **Salty Sow** (p52). Mosey over to the **White Horse** (p54) honky tonk – a legit mix of hipster cool and Texas country – then visit the dive bars along E 6th St.

For a local's day in East Austin, see p44.

🔍 Local Life
East Austin Nightlife (p44)

♥ Best of Austin

Eating
Franklin Barbecue (p49)

Dai Due (p52)

Veracruz All Natural (p49)

Drinking
Whisler's (p53)

Nightlife
White Horse (p54)

Getting There

🚗 **Car** From downtown, take E 7th St to East Austin, crossing beneath the I-35.

🚌 **Bus** From the Red River District downtown, ride bus 4 to E 7th St near Comal St.

🚆 **Train** Take MetroRail 550 east from the Downtown Station (401 E 4th St) to the Plaza Saltillo Station (E 5th St near Comal St).

Local Life
East Austin Nightlife

E 6th St is akin to a Wild West town – right before the politicians moved in to stamp out the fun with their rules and regulations. New residential developments loom over dive bars, craft cocktail bars, worn-out retailers and old houses converted into restaurants. It's a vibrant place to wander at night. In the dives, you'll see more hipsters than hooligans.

❶ Happy Hour Hotspot

The bartenders shine at tiny **Licha's Cantina** (p52), a Mexican restaurant spilling out of an old bungalow. It's an upbeat place to fuel up on margaritas, chips and guacamole before heading out. It's also a favorite hole-in-the-wall for locals, so don't tell anyone we told ya about it. Margaritas are $5 from 4pm to 6pm Tuesday to Friday.

② Destination: Dive Bar

The strip of E 6th St between Onion and Chicon Sts is packed tight with hip dive bars. It's hard to say if one is better than the other, it just depends on who's there on any particular night. See who's playing at **Hotel Vegas** (1502 E 6th St; www.texashotelvegas.com), or step into the dark confines of the **Liberty Bar** (1618 E 6th Ave; www.thelibertyaustin.com) if you want to hide out while sipping your well-crafted Texas Mule.

③ White Horse

Well of course there's a honky-tonk next to a glossy apartment complex. And since this is Austin, it just seems to work. An easy-going bar and mini-dance hall just off 6th St, **White Horse** (p54) is a good place to learn to two-step – it offers lessons before the band starts. There are craft beers aplenty plus whiskey on tap. Patio and food truck too.

④ Craft Cocktail & Thai

Sexy lighting and top-notch libations keep everyone happy – and looking fine – at busy and high-ceilinged **Whisler's** (p53). For one of the best food trucks in town, walk to the back patio and order one of a handful of Thai dishes whipped up inside the colorful **Thai-Kun food truck** (p50), part of the popular East Side King family of Austin restaurants and trailers.

⑤ Cheap & Loud

No, we're not talking about your ex. We're talking about the **Violet Crown Social Club** (p54). With crafts beers, an intimate and dark interior, a dog-friendly patio and an awesome food truck (of course) serving up hearty Detroit-style pizza from **Via 313** (www.via313.com), this is a darn fun place to end the evening.

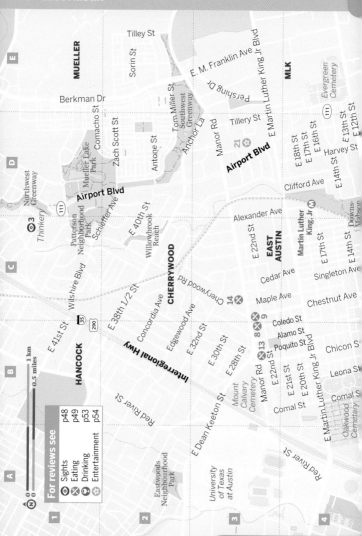

MUELLER

Tilley St

Sorin St

E. M. Franklin Ave

Berkman Dr

Pershing Dr

MLK

Evergreen Cemetery

Comacho St

Zach Scott St

Antone St

Tom Miller St

Southwest Greenway

Anchor La

Manor Rd

Tillery St

E Martin Luther King Jr Blvd

E 18th St

E 17th St

E 16th St

E 13th St

E 12th St

Northwest Greenway

Thinkery 3

Mueller Lake Park

Airport Blvd

Schieffer Ave

E 40th St

Willowbrook Reach

Patterson Neighborhood Park

Airport Blvd

21

Harvey St

E 14th St

Clifford Ave

Alexander Ave

Martin Luther King Jr

Downs- Mabson

Wilshire Blvd

E 41st St

CHERRYWOOD

Cherrywood Rd

E 22nd St

EAST AUSTIN

Martin Luther King Jr

E 17th St

E 14th St

Cedar Ave

Singleton Ave

HANCOCK

E 38th 1/2 St

Concordia Ave

Edgewood Ave

E 32nd St

Maple Ave

14

Chestnut Ave

Coledo St

9

8

Alamo St

13

Poquito St

Chicon S

E 30th St

E 28th St

Manor Rd

E 22nd St

E 21st St

E 20th St

Leona St

Red River St

Mount Calvary Cemetery

Comal St

E Martin Luther King Jr Blvd

Comal S

Oakwood Cemetery

E Dean Keeton St

Eastwoods Neighbourhood Park

University of Texas at Austin

Red River St

1 km

0.5 miles

For reviews see

◉ Sights	p48
✗ Eating	p49
🍷 Drinking	p53
✪ Entertainment	p54

Gunter St
Oak Springs Dr
Airport Blvd (111)
Kirk Ave
⊙ **1** Austin Bouldering Project
Shady La
Mansell Ave

Goodwin Ave
Gunter St
19 ⊗ 19
Springdale Rd
E 7th St ⊗ **15**
E 5th St

Tillery St
Govalle Ave
Cielo St
Neal St
Stokes Dr
GOVALLE
Lyons Rd
Castro St Boggy Creek
Prado St
Garwood St
Gonzales St
E Cesar Chavez St (E 1st St)
Red Bluff Rd
Colorado River

Thompson St
Neal St
N Pleasant Valley Rd
Tillery St
Linden St

Boggy Creek Greenbelt
Nile St
Northwestern Ave
Webberville Rd
Zaragosa Park
N Pleasant Valley Rd
E 5th St
E 3rd St

EAST AUSTIN
E 10th St
E 9th St
E 8th St
E 7th St
Poquito St
Hidalgo St
Santa Maria St
San Saba St
Pedernales St
Canterbury St
Metz Park
The Basin

New York Ave
Pennsylvania Ave
S L Davis Ave
Lincoln St
Chicon St
E 6th St
E 3rd St
Robert Martinez Jr St
HOLLY
Mildred St
⊗ **12**

Comal St
E 13th St
E 12th St
George Washington Carver Museum
⊙ **2**
Rosewood Ave
E 11th St
Concho St
Comal St
Texas State Cemetery
⊙ **4**
16 ⊡
E 5th St
E 4th St
Chicon St
E 1st St
⊗ **6**
Willow St
Anthony St
Lynn St
Holly St
Garden St
Haskell St
Riverview St

Navasota St
Plaza Saltillo
17
E 3rd St
E 2nd St
E Cesar Chavez St (E 1st St)
11 ⊡
20

Branch St
Juniper St
E 11th St
Olive St
Curve St
⊗ **5**
⊗ **10**
E 10th St
Lydia St
E 9th St
E 8th St
⊗ **11**
E 7th St
18
⊙ **9**
Waller St
San Marcos St
⊗ **7**
E Cesar Chavez St
Comal St
Canterbury St
Willow St
EAST CESAR CHAVEZ
Martin Middle School

Navasota St
Interregional Hwy (35)(290)
E 6th St
Lady Bird Lake

E 13th St
E 12th St

47

Sights

Austin Bouldering Project
CLIMBING

1 Map p46, E6

If a fear of ropes and harnesses has kept you from rock climbing, give bouldering a try at this new facility in East Austin. The climbing heights are typically 13ft to 15ft, with a few stretching higher. A thick floor pad will cushion your fall. Bright and airy, the complex has a 2nd-floor viewing area, and the place has a positive and communal vibe. (☑512-645-4633; www.austinboulderingproject. com; 979 Springdale Rd; day pass adult/child $16/12, shoe rental $4; ☺6am-11pm Mon-Fri, 9am-10pm Sat & Sun)

George Washington Carver Museum
MUSEUM

2 Map p46, B5

On 19 June 1865, slaves in Texas were freed pursuant to the Emancipation Proclamation – 2½ years after it was signed by President Lincoln. This day is now honored as Juneteenth, and an exhibit at this small museum examines its history. The museum also holds a few personal items of African American botanist and inventor George Washington Carver. (www. austintexas.gov; 1165 Angelina St; admission free; ☺10am-6pm Mon-Wed, to 9pm Thu, to 5pm Fri, to 4pm Sat; ⊞)

Thinkery
MUSEUM

3 Map p46, C1

This huge 40,000-sq-ft space north of downtown is an inspiring place for young minds, with hands-on activities in the realms of science, technology and the arts. Kids can get learning about fluid dynamics, build LED light structures and explore chemical reactions in the Kitchen Lab, among many other attractions. There's also an outdoor play area with nets and climbing toys. Closed Monday except for Baby Bloomers and other special events. (☑512-469-6200; www.thinkery austin.org; 1830 Simond Ave; $10, child under 2 yrs free; ☺10am-5pm Tue, Thu & Fri, to 8pm Wed, to 6pm Sat & Sun; ⊞)

Texas State Cemetery
CEMETERY

4 Map p46, B6

Revitalized in the 1990s, the state's official cemetery is the final resting place of key figures from Texan history. Interred here are luminaries including Stephen F Austin, Miriam 'Ma' Ferguson (the state's first female governor), writer James Michener and Lone Star State flag designer Joanna Troutman, along with thousands of soldiers who died in the Civil War, plus more than 100 leaders of the Republic of Texas who were exhumed from other sites and reburied here. Self-guided-tour brochures are usually available from the visitor center. The cemetery is just north of E 7th St. (☑512-463-0605; 909

George Washington Carver Museum

Navasota St; ⊙8am-5pm daily, visitor center 8am-5pm Mon-Fri)

Eating

Franklin Barbecue   BARBECUE **$**

 5   Map p46, A5

This famous BBQ joint only serves lunch, and only till it runs out – usually well before 2pm. In fact, to avoid missing out, you should join the line – and there will be a line – by 10am (9am on weekends). Just treat it as a tailgating party: bring beer or mimosas to share and make friends. And yes, you do want the fatty brisket. (☑512-653-1187; www.franklinbarbecue.com; 900 E 11th St; sandwiches $6-10, ribs/brisket per lb $17/20; ⊙11am-2pm Tue-Sun)

Veracruz All Natural   MEXICAN **$**

6   Map p46, B7

Two sisters from Mexico run this East Austin taco truck (an old bus), which may serve the best tacos in town. Step up to the window, order a *migas* breakfast taco (you must!) then add a quesadilla or torta for variety. Take your buzzer – yep, this food truck has a buzzer – and grab a picnic table. (☑512-981-1760; www.veracruztacos.com; 1704 E Caser Chavez St; tacos $3-4, mains $8; ⊙7am-3pm)

Understand

BBQ in Lockhart

The city of Lockhart may be be 30 miles southeast of Austin, but when you're talking about a place that's home to four outstanding BBQ restaurants, a short drive is not an issue. How good is Lockhart? Well, in 1999, the Texas Legislature adopted a resolution naming Lockhart the barbecue capital of Texas. Of course, that means it's the barbecue capital of the world. You can eat very well for under $15.

Black's Barbecue (☎512-398-2712; www.blacksbbq.com; 215 N Main St; sandwiches $10-13, brisket per lb $16.50; ☺10am-8pm Sun-Thu, to 8:30pm Fri & Sat) A longtime Lockhart favorite since 1932, with sausage so good Lyndon Johnson had them cater a party at the nation's capital.

Kreuz Market (☎512-398-2361; www.kreuzmarket.com; 619 N Colorado St; brisket per lb $16.49; ☺10:30am-8pm Mon-Sat, to 6pm Sun) Serving Lockhart since 1900, the barnlike Kreuz Market uses a dry rub, which means you shouldn't insult them by asking for barbecue sauce; they don't serve it, and the meat doesn't need it.

Chisholm Trail Bar-B-Q (☎512-398-6027; www.lockhartchisolmtrailbbq.com; 1323 S Colorado St; lunch plates $8-13, brisket per lb $13.50; ☺8am-8pm Sun-Wed, 6am-9pm Thu-Sat) Like Black's and Kreuz, Chisholm Trail has been named one of the top 10 barbecue restaurants in the state by Texas Monthly magazine. Has a drive-through if you're in a hurry.

Smitty's Market (☎512-398-9344; www.smittysmarket.com; 208 S Commerce St; brisket per lb $14.90; ☺7am-6pm Mon-Fri, to 6:30pm Sat, 9am-6:30pm Sun) The blackened pit room and homely dining room are all original (knives used to be chained to the tables). Ask them to trim off the fat on the brisket if you're particular about that.

Thai-Kun at Whisler's   THAI $

The beef panang curry is, simply put, amazing. Served from a colorful food truck behind Whisler's cocktail bar (see 16 🚇 Map p46, B6), this spicy curry is one of a half-dozen noodle and curry dishes on the menu, all under the oversight of chef Thai Changdong. The food truck was named one of the best new restaurants in America by *Bon Appetit!* (☎512-719-3332; www.thaikun.com; 1816 E 6th St; mains $7-10; ☺4pm-1:45am)

Cenote

CAFE $

7 Map p46, A7

One of our favorite cafes in Austin, Cenote uses seasonal, largely organic ingredients in its simple but delicious anytime fare. Come for housemade granola and yogurt with fruit, banh mi sandwiches and couscous curry. The cleverly shaded patio is a fine retreat for a rich coffee or a craft beer (or perhaps a handmade popsicle from Juju). (1010 E Cesar Chavez St; mains $8-15; 7am-10pm Mon-Fri, from 8am Sat, 8am-4pm Sun;)

Mi Madre's

MEXICAN $

8 Map p46, B3

Barbacoa, chorizo and *adobado* are just a few of the authentic Mexican specialties here. In fact, it was recommended by a friend who said the *barbacoa* was just like his grandma used to make. Praise doesn't come much higher than that. Before dinner, enjoy a drink at the brand-new mezcal bar on the roof. (512-322-9721; www.mimadresrestaurant.com; 2201 Manor Rd; tacos $3-5, mains $9-14; 6am-2pm Mon & Tue, to 10pm Wed-Sat, 8am-4pm Sun)

El Chilito

TEX-MEX $

9 Map p46, C3

If you want quick, cheap and easy, this walk-up taco stand (with a big deck for your dining pleasure) can't be beat. You've got to try breakfast tacos while you're in Austin, and this is a good place to get them. (512-382-3797; www.elchilito.com; 2219 Manor Rd; tacos & burritos $3-9; 7am-10pm Mon-Fri, from 8am Sat & Sun)

Paperboy

AMERICAN, BREAKFAST $

10 Map p46, A6

Even the food trucks here are going hyper local, 'curating' menus based on what's available. Breakfast wunderkind Paperboy does this particularly well, luring in-the-know locals with gourmet breakfast sandwiches. A recent menu featured

 Local Life
Heading out in East Austin

Bar-hopping on E 6th St The block east of I-35 turns vibrant as the sun goes down and the dive bars and eateries fill with hip and festive crowds.

Farm to Table Fare Austin foodies rave about the carefully crafted dishes that embrace regional bounty, from wild game at Dai Due (p52) to the pork at Salty Sow (p52), to the locally sourced breakfast at Paperboy food truck.

Neighborhood Dining & Drinking Insiders have long loved the traditional Mexican dishes at Mi Madre's, but now they keep the party going at the new mescal bar upstairs

Top Tip

Whisler's

With fantastic craft cocktails, skilled service and flattering lighting, it would be easy to call it a night – a good night – after spending an hour at the bar in Whisler's (p53), or checking out a band on the adjacent and festive patio. But also visit the small backyard. That's where you'll find some of the best Thai food in the city – delicious and spicy noodles and curries all served up from the colorful Thai-Kun (p50) food truck.

an egg-covered pimiento cheese and bacon sandwich and a sweet-potato hash with braised pork belly and kale. (www.paperboyaustin.com; 1203 E 11th St; mains $7-9; ⏱7am-2pm Tue-Fri, 8am-2pm Sat & Sun)

Licha's Cantina　　MEXICAN $$

 11　　Map p46, A6

This cozy cottage may lure you in with its $5 drink specials at happy hour (4pm to 6pm Tuesday to Friday), but the interior Mexican dishes will have you sticking around. Eat inside, or in the yard out front, or settle in at the bar where the conversations are intriguing and the service top-notch. (www.lichascantina.com; 1306 E 6th St; mains $13-27; ⏱4-11pm Tue-Thu, 4pm-midnight Fri, noon-midnight Sat, 11am-3pm Sun)

Laundrette　　MODERN AMERICAN $$

12　　Map p46, B8

A brilliant repurposing of a former washeteria, Laundrette boasts a stylish, streamlined design that provides a fine backdrop to the delicious Mediterranean-inspired cooking. Among the many hits: crab toast, wood-grilled octopus, brussels sprouts with apple-bacon marmalade, a perfectly rendered brick chicken and whole grilled branzino. (☑512-382-1599; 2115 Holly St; mains $18-24; ⏱11am-2:30pm daily, 5-10pm Sun-Thu, to 11pm Fri & Sat)

Salty Sow　　AMERICAN $$

13　　Map p46, B3

Behold the porcine wonder! This snout-to-tail restaurant advertising 'swine + wine' offers a thoroughly modern take on down-home cooking, including plenty of choices in the nonpork category. (☑512-391-2337; www.saltysow.com; 1917 Manor Rd; small plates $8-12, mains $16-24; ⏱4:30-10pm Sun-Thu, to 11pm Fri & Sat)

Dai Due　　AMERICAN $$$

14　　Map p46, C3

Even your basic eggs-and-sausage breakfast is a meal to remember at this lauded restaurant, where all the ingredients are from farms, rivers and hunting grounds in Texas, as well as the Gulf of Mexico. Supper Club dinners spotlight limited items like wild game and foraged treats. Like your cut of meat? See if they have

East Austin bar

a few pounds to-go at the attached butcher shop. (📞512-719-3332; www. daidue.com; 2406 Manor Rd; breakfast & lunch $13-22, dinner $22-84; ⏰10am-3pm & 5-10pm Tue-Sun)

Justine's

FRENCH $$$

15 🍴 Map p46, E8

With a lovely garden setting festooned with fairy lights, Justine's is a top spot for wowing a date. French onion soup, seared scallops and grilled pork chop are standouts on the small, classic brasserie menu. There are also a few more creative changing daily specials like panseared quail with parsnip casserole or grilled swordfish with artichokes

and cauliflower puree. (📞512-385-2900; www.justines1937.com; 4710 E 5th St; mains $20-28; ⏰6pm-2am Wed-Mon)

Drinking

Whisler's

COCKTAIL BAR

16 🍸 Map p46, B6

If vampires walk the streets of East Austin, then this dark and moody cocktail bar is surely where they congregate before a night of feeding. And we don't quite trust that taxidermied boar overlooking the bar from his lofty perch. Head to the patio for a less intimate scene, as well as live music. There's a fantastic

Thai food truck out back. (☎512-480-0781; www.whislersatx.com; 1816 E 6th St; ⏱4pm-2am)

White Horse HONKY-TONK

17 Map p46, B6

Ladies, you will be asked to dance at this East Austin honky-tonk, where two-steppers and hipsters mingle like siblings in a diverse but happy family. Play pool, take a dance lesson or step outside to sip a microbrew on the patio. Live music nightly, and whiskey on tap. We like this place. (☎512-553-6756; www.thewhitehorseaustin.com; 500 Comal St; ⏱3pm-2am)

Violet Crown Social Club BAR

18 Map p46, A6

It's dark. It's loud. At first glance it's not terribly inviting. But damn, the drinks are cheap, making this a popular spot on the East 6th circuit. (1111 E 6th St; ⏱5pm-2am)

Sa-Ten Coffee & Eats COFFEE

19 Map p46, E7

If you're on the east side of town and need a caffeine jolt, head to this bright and minimalist box for top-notch coffees and a small menu of Japanese snacks. This busy place is tucked among galleries and studios

in the Canopy Austin artist complex. There are outside tables if you need some sunshine. (☎512-524-1544; www.sa-ten.com; 916 Springdale Rd; ⏱7am-10pm; 🛜)

Flat Track Coffee COFFEE

20 Map p46, B7

This East Austin java joint also houses a bicycle repair shop. Or maybe it's the other way around. Either way, this former coffee-catering company is the go-to spot for coffee aficionados east of the I-35. On weekends, you'll find a food truck out front selling mini-donuts. Cycles also for rent. (☎512-814-6010; www.flattrackcoffee.com; 1619 E Cesar Chavez St; ⏱7am-7pm)

Entertainment

Skylark Lounge BLUES

21 ⭐ Map p46, D3

It's a bit of a drive (2.5 miles northeast of downtown), but well worth the effort to reach this friendly dive bar that serves up live blues – along with fairly priced drinks, free popcorn and a shaded patio. (☎512-730-0759; www.skylarkaustin.com; 2039 Airport Blvd; ⏱5pm-midnight Mon-Fri, to 1am Sat, to 10pm Sun)

Hearty fare at Franklin Barbecue (p49)

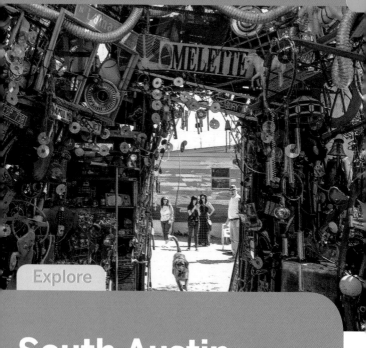

Explore

South Austin

This quirky but festive neighborhood – especially along S Congress Ave – is the city's soul. Tourism types nicknamed it SoCo, which has somewhat stuck, but locals mostly call it South Congress. The road is the main thoroughfare through the neighborhood and the epicenter of the action; most of the rest is residential, although burgeoning S 1st St has been been seeing more commercial activity in recent years.

The Sights in a Day

☀ Savor a croissant and Vietnamese coffee at **Elizabeth Street Cafe** (p73). Check out the nearby murals then head to **Zilker Park** (p60) for an invigorating dip in spring-fed **Barton Springs Pool** (p79). Not up for a swim? Then check out the animals in the **nature & science center** (p61) or stroll past the statues in the **UMLAUF Sculpture Garden & Museum** (p61).

☀ Take your pick of awesome taco spots for lunch then stroll S Congress Ave to try on cowboy boots at **Allens Boots** (p65) and peruse one-of-a-kind- antiques at **Uncommon Objects** (p65). Take a coffee break at **Jo's Coffee** (p74) and take the obligatory snap in front of the **I Love You So Much mural** (p68) on the side of the building. Cocktails on the patio of the adjacent **Hotel San José** (p73) are a pleasant respite too.

☽ Join the line for a topping-slathered burger at **Hopdoddy Burger Bar** (p71) then choose your evening entertainment: live music at the **Continental Club** (p74) across the street from Jo's, or take a short drive to the **Broken Spoke** (p74) for two-stepping to live Texas country tunes.

For a local's day in South Austin, see p64.

Left: Cathedral of Junk (p70) by Vince Hanneman

 Top Sights

Bat Colony Under the Congress Avenue Bridge (p58)

Zilker Park (p60)

Lady Bird Johnson Wildflower Center (p62)

 Local Life

South Congress Stroll (p64)

💜 **Best of Austin**

Eating
Hopdoddy Burger Bar (p71)

Drinking
Hotel San José (p73)

Entertainment
Broken Spoke (p74)

Shopping
Uncommon Objects (p65)

Getting There

🚗 **Car** From downtown, follow Congress Ave south over Lady Bird Lake.

🚲 **Bike** There are three B-cycle stations on S Congress Ave.

🚌 **Bus** Bus 1 connects S Congress Ave with downtown then travels along Lavaca St to Guadalupe St near UT to N Lamar Blvd.

Top Sights
Bat Colony Under the Congress Avenue Bridge

Looking very much like a special effect from a B movie, a funnel cloud of up to 1.5 million Mexican free-tailed bats swarms from under the Congress Avenue Bridge nightly from late March to early November. Turns out Austin isn't just the live-music capital of the world; it's also home to the largest urban bat population in North America.

👁 Map p66, G1

Congress Ave

🕒 sunset Apr-Nov

Watching the swarm from a Lone Star Riverboat and Congress Avenue Bridge

Bat Story

The Congress Avenue Bridge was built in 1910. After improvements to the bridge in 1980, a colony of Mexican free-tailed bats moved in. Apparently the bats like the bridge's nooks and crannies for roosting. These tiny winged mammals live in Mexico in the winter then migrate north when Austin warms up. They typically swarm out at twilight to feed. The colony is made up entirely of female and young animals. Such is the bat-density that bat-radars have detected bat-columns up to 10,000ft (3,050m) high. In June, each female gives birth to one pup, and every night at dusk, the families take to the skies in search of food.

Bat Viewing from Land

It's become an Austin tradition to head to Lady Bird Lake to watch the bats swarm out to feed on an estimated 10,000lb to 20,000lb of insects per night. The swarm looks a lot like a fast-moving, black, chittering river. Best places on land for viewing? One easy spot is the sidewalk on the eastern side of the bridge. You can also try the grassy lawn behind the Austin-American Statesman building at 305 S Congress Ave, on the southeast end of the bridge. Parking in the Statesman lot is $6 for four hours. Don't miss this nightly show. The best viewing is in August.

Bat Cruises & Kayak Tours

To add a little adventure to your bat watching, view the bats from a boat or kayak on Lady Bird Lake. During bat season, **Lone Star Riverboat** (☏512-327-1388; www.lonestarriverboat.com; adult/child $10/7; ☉Mar–mid-Dec) offers nightly sunset bat-watching trips on its 32ft electric cruiser. **Capital Cruises** (☏512-480-9264; www.capitalcruises.com; adult/child $10/5) also runs tours. **Live Love Paddle** (www.livelovepaddle) and **Congress Avenue Kayaks** (www.congresskayaks.com) offer guided evening bat tours.

☑ Top Tips

▶ To find out what time the bats will probably emerge during your visit, call the **Bat Hotline** at ☏512-327-9721 ext 3.

✗ Take a Break

Many good restaurants line S Congress Ave south of the bridge. For Tex-Mex and a lively scene, head to Güero's Taco Bar (p73).

For ice cream, try Amy's Ice Creams (p70) where they'll mix – or smash – your choice of toppings into your scoops.

Top Sights
Zilker Park

Established through a series of gifts by local businessman Andrew Jackson Zilker, this 350-acre park is a slice of green heaven, lined with hiking and biking trails. It celebrated its 100th birthday in 2017. The park also provides access to the famed Barton Springs (p79) natural swimming pool and Barton Creek Greenbelt (p68). Other attractions include a botanical garden, kayak rentals, a nature center, disc golf and a miniature train.

 Map p66, B1

512-974-6700

www.austintexas.gov/department/zilker-metropolitan-park

2100 Barton Springs Rd

5am-10pm

Charles Umlauf, *The Kiss*, 1970, bronze, cast in Italy

Barton Springs Pool

Hot? Not for long. Even when the temperature hits 100, you'll be shivering in a jiff after you jump into this icy-cold natural-spring pool (p79). The pool is fed by the Edwards Aquifer, which flows to the springs through limestone channels. The Moderne-style bathhouse was built in 1947. Draped with century-old pecan trees, the area around the pool is a social scene in itself, and the place gets packed on hot summer days.

Zilker Botanical Garden

These lush **gardens** (☎512-477-8672; www.zilkergarden.
org; 2220 Barton Springs Rd; adult/child $3/1; ☺9am-5pm,
to 7pm during daylight saving time) cover 31 acres on the south bank of Lady Bird Lake, with displays including natural grottoes, a Japanese garden and a fragrant herb garden. You'll also find interesting historical artifacts sprinkled about the site, including a 19th-century pioneer cabin.

UMLAUF Sculpture Garden & Museum

If the weather's just too perfect to be inside, stroll the open-air **UMLAUF Sculpture Garden & Museum** (☎512-445-5582; www.umlaufsculpture.org; 605 Robert
E Lee Rd; adult/child under 12yr/student $5/free/1; ☺10am-
4pm Tue-Fri, noon-4pm Sat & Sun) in the southern end of the park. Within the sculpture garden and the indoor museum there are more than 130 works by 20th-century American sculptor Charles Umlauf, who was an art professor at UT for 40 years.

Austin Nature & Science Center

In the northwestern area of the park, the **Austin Nature & Science Center** (☎512-974-3888; www.
austintexas.gov/department/austin-nature-science-center;
301 Nature Center Dr; donations requested; ☺9am-5pm
Mon-Sat, noon-5pm Sun) has exhibitions of native Texan mammals, birds, reptiles, amphibians and arthropods.

☑ **Top Tips**

▶ To get out on the lake, rent a kayak or canoe with **Zilker Park Boat Rentals** (☎512-478-3852; www.zilkerboats.com; 2101 Andrew Zilker Rd; per hr/day $15/45; ☺10am-dusk). To find the rental facility, turn left immediately after entering the park from Barton Springs Rd. The canoes are below the parking lot, on the shore of the creek. Look for the 'Canoe Rental is Open' banner.

▶ On weekends from April to early September, admission is $5 per car. The $3 admission fee for Zilker Botanical Garden is cash or check only.

✗ **Take a Break**

After wandering the sculpture or botanical gardens, drive to Elizabeth Street Cafe (p73) for a light French-Vietnamese lunch or a pastry.

Top Sights
Lady Bird Johnson Wildflower Center

Anyone with an interest in Texas' flora and fauna should make the 20-minute drive to the wonderful gardens of the Lady Bird Johnson Wildflower Center, southwest of downtown Austin. The center, founded in 1982 with the assistance of Texas' beloved former first lady, has a display garden featuring every type of wildflower and plant that grows in Texas, separated by geographical region, with an emphasis on Hill Country flora.

Map p66, A5

512-232-0100

www.wildflower.org

4801 La Crosse Ave

adult/child 5-17yr/student & senior $10/4/8

9am-5pm Tue-Sun

Bluebonnets at the Wildflower Center

Lady Bird Johnson

Lady Bird Johnson's belief that beautiful surroundings could boost the morale and mental health of Americans was the force behind her national beautification efforts during her husband Lyndon B Johnson's presidency. She created the National Wildflower Research Center in 1982 with actress Helen Hayes. It outgrew its original East Austin home, moving to its current location in 1995, and was renamed in her honor two years later.

Central Gardens

These sustainable gardens showcase many of the 650 species of native plants found across the 284-acre center. Sustainable plants don't harm the environment and actually help to sustain it through various methods that ultimately conserve water, support wildlife and otherwise help the surrounding ecosystem. The pollinator habitat garden, for instance, is an open-air garden created to attract and support butterflies and other pollinators.

Family Garden

This is a pretty place to let youngsters explore, learn and blow off steam, with the added bonus of a gorgeous backdrop for parents to enjoy. Immersive features in this 4.5-acre garden include a shrub maze, a lazy creek, a tree 'stumpery' with giant stumps, and a grotto with caves and a waterfall.

Texas Arboretum

If you enjoy history, take a moment to walk to the Hall of Trees in the Texas Arboretum. It's a large circle of live oaks, each descended from a famous tree. The explanatory panels provide details about each tree, describing its impeccable heritage and illustrious forebear – it's the family tree for an actual tree!

☑ Top Tips

▶ Spring is the best time to visit, but there's something in bloom all year.

▶ Check the website before your visit to see what flowers are in season.

▶ Stretch your legs on 2 miles of trails.

▶ The Wildflower Center hosts a variety of events during National Wildflower Week in May.

✗ Take a Break

On-site, the **Wildflower Cafe** serves salads, sandwiches and hibiscus mint iced tea. A few kids' options are available too.

For a drink in an aesthetically pleasing spot in South Austin, take a seat on the patio at the Hotel San José (p73).

Local Life
South Congress Stroll

You won't find any chain stores along S Congress Ave, and the indie shops here are truly unique. Which explains the heavy flow of pedestrians filling those sidewalks on weekends and on weekday evenings. Cafes, coffee shops and dessert spots are also temptingly easy to find. People-watching is superb.

....

❶ **Costume Central**
If you want to get a jump on your costume shopping for Halloween, **Lucy in Disguise** (p76) is the place to go. Outfits and costumes are arranged by genre, from burlesque to Ancient Rome, and by decade, including the '70s, baby. It's a fun place to start a stroll, with costumes and occasionally wacky vintage duds highlighting the joyful weirdness of Austin.

❷ Antiques Here, There and Everywhere

Take a breath. You're going to be spending some time in **Uncommon Objects** (☎512-442-4000; 1512 S Congress Ave; ⏰11am-7pm Sun-Thu, to 8pm Fri & Sat), an enticing antique mall where more than 20 vendors show off a packed-tight array of antiques. Many of these finds would look right at home in your rustic chic digs back home.

❸ Boots Galore

Be careful in here. Looking at the towering aisles of men's and women's cowboy boots – all arranged by shoe size – at **Allens Boots** (☎512-447-1413; 1522 S Congress Ave; ⏰9am-8pm Mon-Sat, noon-6pm Sun) is akin to looking at puppies. It's hard to leave empty-handed; you *are* in Texas after all. Makers include Lucchese, Justin, Tony Lama and Frye. Hats and accessories sold here too.

❹ Candy, Candy, Candy

Willy Wonka would be impressed by **Big Top Candy Shop** (www.bigtopcandy shop.tumblr.com; 1706 S Congress Ave; ⏰11am-7pm Sun-Thu, 11am-8pm Fri, 10am-9pm Sat; 👪), a narrow store that manages to cram in an amazing array of sweet delights, from old-school classics to modern favorites. The array of gummy treats is astounding. Also sells ice cream. For bulk purchases, head to the bins and scoops in back.

❺ Coffee, Style and Hospitality

Walk across S Congress Ave to check out the sleek new **South Congress Hotel** (www.southcongresshotel.com; 1603 S Congress Ave; r/ste from $352/640; 🛜🐾🍸). And while the decor is minimalist cool, we swear this place has the nicest doormen around. Inside, the gift shop has a few unique finds and you'll see a couple of good patios for snacking and people-watching. Or grab an iced coffee at Café No Sé. Motorcycle enthusiasts dig the bikes at Revival Cycles (www.revivalcycles. com), where the handcrafted rides could double as works of art. Make that *badass* art, of course.

❻ Treat Yourself at Tesoros

Continue back up S Congress Ave, crossing over to **Tesoros Trading Co** (☎512-447-7500; 1500 S Congress Ave; ⏰11am-6pm Sun-Fri, 10am-6pm Sat). Well-stocked with colorful and unique arts-and-crafts, many with a Latin influence, it's a good spot for an end-of-stroll personal reward.

A **B** **C** **D**

Zilker
Park

1

2 Barton Creek
Greenbelt

Barton Creek

15

Barton Creek

Barton Springs Rd

Barton Creek

Barton
Springs

Virginia Ave

BARTON
HILLS

Barton Hills Dr

Robert E Lee Rd

Lund St

Kerr St

Barton Blvd

Lindscomb Ave

Garrider Ave

Kinney Ave

Juliet St

2

Bluebonnet La

Folts Ave

Dexter St

Treadwell St

Ethel St

Jessie St

Margaret St

Treadwell St

Dexter St

27

Dwyer Ave

Ashby Ave

Oxford Ave

Lamar
Square Dr

14

3

0   500 m
0   0.25 miles

Anita Dr

Ford St

ZILKER

Collier St

29

Paramount Ave

Ann Arbor Ave

Bluebonnet La

Nash Ave

Bauerle Ave

Kinney Ave

Hether St

SouthPop
9

S Lamar Blvd

S 7th St

Rabb Rd

De Verne St

Rabb Glen St

Goodrich Ave

Oxford Ave

S 6th St

S 5th St

Arpdale St

4

31

37

*Ricky
Guerrero
Park*

La Casa Dr

S Lamar Blvd

Del Curto Rd

Thornton Rd

23

W Oltorf St

Southwood Rd

S 5th St

W Live Oak

11

5

25

**Lady Bird Johnson
Wildflower Center**
(9mi)

**SOUTH
LAMAR**

Fieldcrest Dr

*South Austin
Neighborhood
Park*

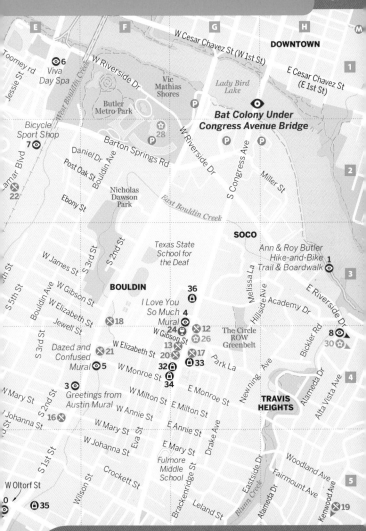

E   F   G   H   M

W Cesar Chavez St (W 1st St)

DOWNTOWN

E Cesar Chavez St
(E 1st St)

1

Toomey rd
Jessie St
⊙6
Viva
Day Spa

W Riverside Dr

West Bouldin Creek

Vic
Mathias
Shores

*Lady Bird
Lake*

**Bat Colony Under
Congress Avenue Bridge**

Bicycle
Sport Shop
7⊙

Butler
Metro Park

P

P

Barton Springs Rd

⊛28

W Riverside Dr

P

P

S Congress Ave

Miller St

2

Daniel Dr
Post Oak St
Bouldin Ave

W Lamar Blvd
⊠
22

Ebony St

Nicholas
Dawson
Park

East Bouldin Creek

SOCO

Ann & Roy Butler
Hike-and-Bike
Trail & Boardwalk 1⊙

3

S 5th St
W James St
S 3rd St
S 2nd St

Texas State
School for
the Deaf

Melissa La
Hillside Ave
Academy Dr

E Riverside Dr

Bouldin Ave
W Gibson St
W Elizabeth St
Jewell St
⊠18

BOULDIN

36
🔒

*I Love You
So Much*
Mural 4⊙

24⊠
13⊠
20⊠

⊠12
26🅿

W Gibson St

The Circle
ROW
Greenbelt

8⊙
30⊛

Bickler Rd

S 3rd St
Dazed and
Confused
Mural ⊙5

⊠21

W Elizabeth St

32🔒
34

⊠17
33🔒

Park La

Newning Ave

Alameda Dr
Alta Vista Ave

4

N Mary St
S 2nd St

3⊙
*Greetings from
Austin Mural*

16⊠

W Monroe St
E Monroe St

W Milton St E Milton St
W Annie St
S Johanna St
W Mary St Eva St
E Annie St
W Johanna St

E Mary St

Fulmore
Middle
School

**TRAVIS
HEIGHTS**

Eastside Dr

Woodland Ave
Fairmount Ave

Alameda Dr

5

S 1st St
W Oltorf St
0

🔒35

Wilson St
Crockett St

Brackenridge St

Leland St

Blunn Creek

Alameda Dr

Kenwood Ave
⊠19

Sights

Ann & Roy Butler Hike-and-Bike Trail & Boardwalk
VIEWPOINT, ARCHITECTURE

1 Map p66, H3

You can gaze at the downtown skyline from a series of photogenic boardwalks on this scenic 10-mile trail, which loops around Lady Bird Lake. Shorten the loop by crossing the lake on one of several bridges. You'll find restrooms, water fountains and waste bags for your pet along the way. Check the city's Parks & Recreation webpage (www.austintexas.gov/department/parks-and-recreation) for parking lots, trail access points and ADA accessible entrances. Austin old-timers may refer to the trail as the Lady Bird Trail or the Town Lake Trail. (www.austintexas.gov; 1820 Lakeshore Blvd; ⊙5am-midnight; 👫 🐾)

Barton Creek Greenbelt
PARK

2 Map p66, B1

From Zilker Park, this refreshing multiuse path unfurls for more than 8 miles along Barton Creek. Hike, bike and splash around. There are several access points, including the entry path near 1601 Spyglass Rd. Leashed dogs OK. (www.austintexas.gov; 3753 S Capital of Texas Hwy)

Greetings from Austin Mural
PUBLIC ART

3 Map p66, E4

Well of course you're going to pull over and take a photo in front of this wall-sized postcard. It's awesome. The eye-catching mural adorns the south-side of the Roadhouse Relics building. (1720 S 1st St)

I Love You So Much Mural
PUBLIC ART

4 Map p66, G3

This simple expression of devotion draws legions of photo-taking love-birds. Spray-painted on the side of Jo's Coffee on South Congress, it now joins the Austin Motel sign and the patio at Guero's as an iconic symbol of the neighborhood. Eagle-eyed visitors may spot funny spin-offs of the mural around town. (1300 S Congress Ave)

 Top Tip

A Congress Ave Alternative: S 1st Street

If you tire of the crowds on S Congress Ave, take a walk or drive to nearby S 1st St. This burgeoning strip is filling up quickly with coffee shops and indie-owned eateries that rival their better-known neighbors in quality and style. For coffee, give scrappy Bouldin Creek Coffee House (p71) a try. Elizabeth Street Cafe (p73) is a great stop for French pastries or tasty *Banh mi*.

Greetings from Austin mural, by artists Rory Skagen and Bill Brakhage

Dazed and Confused Mural

PUBLIC ART

5 ⦿ Map p66, F4

Alright, alright, alright. Fans of Matthew McConaughey and *Dazed and Confused* can pay their respects to Wooderson – the unrepentant admirer of high school girls – at this eye-catching mural a short walk south from Monroe St, near the food truck park. (S 1st St, near Monroe St)

Viva Day Spa

SPA

6 ⦿ Map p66, E1

Repeatedly named 'Best Spa' in the *Austin Chronicle's* Best of Austin awards, Viva is conveniently located downtown so you can steal a few moments of pampering during your visit. (☎512-300-2256; www.vivadayspa.com; 215 S Lamar Blvd; ⊗9am-8pm)

Bicycle Sport Shop

CYCLING

7 ⦿ Map p66, E2

The great thing about Bicycle Sport Shop is its proximity to Zilker Park, Barton Springs and the Lady Bird Lake bike paths, all of which are within a few blocks. Rentals range from $16 for a two-hour cruise on a standard bike, to $62 for a full day on a top-end full-suspension model. On weekends and holidays, advance reservations are advised. (☎512-477-3472; www.bicyclesportshop.com; 517 S Lamar Blvd;

Local Life

Food Culture

Debating Tacos There's no better way to start a conversation than to ask a local which restaurant serves the best tacos. Two perennial favorites are Torchy's Tacos (p72) and Tacodeli. Torchy's has the mouthwatering fillings while Tacodeli brings it home with its dona sauce. In our opinion, a taste test is a win-win situation.

Late Night Munchies For a cheap eats late at night, head to the takeout window at long-time favorite Home Slice for, well, a slice to take home. Or eat on the sidewalk.

per 2hr from $16; ⏱10am-7pm Mon-Fri, 9am-6pm Sat, 11am-5pm Sun)

Roy G Guerrero Disc Golf Course
GOLF

8 Map p66, H4

A newer course with 18 holes suitable for beginners and skilled players alike. (517 S Pleasant Valley Rd; admission free; ⏱sunrise–sunset)

SouthPop
CULTURAL CENTER

9 ◎ Map p66, D3

Pop into this South Austin gallery for rotating exhibits that spotlight Austin's live music and entertainment scenes, from the 1960s to the present. One recent exhibit celebrated the city's punk rock bands. (South Austin Popular Cultural Center; ☎512-440-8318; www.southpop.org; 1516-B S Lamar Ave; admission free; ⏱1-6pm Thu-Sun)

Cathedral of Junk
SCULPTURE

10 ◎ Map p66, E5

An ongoing (and climbable!) backyard sculpture that turns one man's trash into everyone's treasure. Visitation is by appointment, by phone. Owner Vince Hanneman doesn't always get to his voicemail, so keep trying until he answers. He'll fill you in on parking. Note that you can't really see the cathedral from a drive-by. (☎512-299-7413; 4422 Lareina Dr; requested donation per group $10; ⏱by appointment)

Veloway Track
CYCLING

11 ◎ Map p66, A5

Plan some extra time to ride or skate the great 3.1-mile Veloway track, near the Lady Bird Johnson Wildflower Center. The track runs clockwise, and no walking or running is permitted. (www.veloway.com; 4900 La Crosse Ave; admission free; ⏱dawn-dusk)

Eating

Amy's Ice Creams - South Austin
ICE CREAM $

12 ✕ Map p66, G4

The South Congress location of this beloved local ice-cream chain shares its daily flavors on a chalkboard out front. Pick your favorite add-on, and they'll pound it into your ice-cream choice. (📞512-440-7488; www.amysicecreams.com; 1301 S Congress; ice cream $3.25-6; ⏱11:30am-11pm Sun-Thu, to midnight Fri & Sat)

Hopdoddy Burger Bar   BURGERS $

13 Map p66, G4

People line up around the block for the burgers, fries and shakes – and it's not because burgers, fries and shakes are hard to come by in Austin. It's because this place slathers tons of love into everything it makes, from the humanely raised beef to the locally sourced ingredients to the fresh-baked buns. The sleek, modern building is pretty sweet, too. (📞512-243-7505; www.hopdoddy.com; 1400 S Congress Ave; burgers $7-13; ⏱11am-10pm Sun-Thu, to 11pm Fri & Sat)

Ramen Tatsu-ya   RAMEN $

14 Map p66, D3

With its communal tables, loud indie music and hustling efficiency, we wouldn't say this busy ramen joint is a relaxing experience, but darn is it good. Step up to the counter – there will be a line – and take your pick of seven noodle-and-veggie-loaded broths. Like it spicy? Order the Mi-So-Hot. You can also add spicy or sweet 'bombs' to vary the flavor. (📞512-893-5561; www.ramen-tatsuya.com; 1234 S Lamar Blvd; ramen $10; ⏱11am-10pm)

Tacodeli   TEX-MEX $

15 Map p66, C1

Oh Tacodeli, how we love your handcrafted tacos – surely blessed with the smiles of angels. From the Tacoloco with its adobo-braised brisket to the Pollo Fantistico with its shredded chicken and crema Mexican, the tacos are fresh, local and a touch gourmet. And you simply can't leave without trying the self-serve creamy dona sauce – it has kick. Order at the counter. (📞512-732-0303; www.tacodeli.com; 1500 Spyglass Dr; ⏱7am-3pm Mon-Fri, 8am-3pm Sat & Sun)

Bouldin Creek Coffee House   VEGETARIAN $

16 Map p66, E4

You can get veggie chorizo tacos or a potato leek omelet all day long at this buzzing vegan-vegetarian eatery. It's got an eclectic South Austin vibe and is a great place for people-watching, finishing your novel or joining a band. (📞512-416-1601; www.bouldincreekcafe.com; 1900 S 1st St; mains $6-10; ⏱7am-midnight Mon-Fri, 8am-midnight Sat & Sun; 🛜🅿)

Home Slice   PIZZA $

17 Map p66, G4

Everybody knows about Home Slice. And on Saturday night between 6pm and midnight, it seems everybody is in fact here! All of them digging into the New York–style pies. (📞512-444-7437; www.homeslicepizza.com; 1415 S Congress

Yard Dog (p76)

Ave; slice $4, pizzas $15-22; ⊙11am-11pm Sun, Mon, Wed & Thu, to midnight Fri & Sat)

Torchy's Tacos

TEX-MEX $

18 Map p66, F3

At the South Austin Trailer Park location, they'll tell you what you should be ordering if they think you're making the wrong choice. We like your initiative Torchy's! This long-time favorite, which now has brick-and-mortar locations across the state, was former President Obama's pick on a 2016 Austin visit. His tacos of choice? The Democrat, the Republican and the Independent, we hear. (☏512-916-9235; www. torchystacos.com; 1311 S 1st St; tacos $3-5;

⊙7am-10pm Mon-Thu, 7am-11pm Fri, 8am-11pm Sat, 8am-10pm Sun)

Whip In

INDIAN $

19 Map p66, H5

It started as a convenience store on a frontage road. Then the beer and Indian food started to take over. Now it's part Indian restaurant, part bar and part beer store, with a few groceries still hanging around to keep it confusing. Would we mention it if the food (breakfast naan and 'panaani' sandwiches) wasn't awesome? We would not. (☏512-442-5337; www.whipin. com; 1950 S I-35; breakfast $7-9, brunch, lunch & dinner $9-14; ⊙10am-11pm Sun-Mon, to midnight Tue-Sat)

Güero's Taco Bar

TEX-MEX $$

20 Map p66, G4

Set in a former feed-and-seed store from the late 1800s, Güero's is an Austin classic and always draws a crowd. It may not serve the best Tex-Mex in town but with its free chips and salsa, refreshing margaritas and convivial vibe, we can almost guarantee a fantastic time. And the food? Try the homemade corn tortillas and chicken tortilla soup. (512-447-7688; www.gueros. com; 1412 S Congress Ave; breakfast $5-7, lunch & dinner $10-34; 11am-10pm Mon-Wed, to 11pm Thu & Fri, 8am-11pm Sat, to 10pm Sun)

Elizabeth Street Cafe

FRENCH, VIETNAMESE $$

21 Map p66, F4

We're going to irritate some locals by highlighting this dapper cottage of deliciousness. Pop in for croissants, crepes and a few noodle dishes in the morning, plus the deliciously creamy Vietnamese coffee. And the banh mi? Available all day, these soft baguettes are loaded with bewitchingly tasty fillings. Later in the day look for pho, bun and more Vietnamese house specialties. (512-291-2882; www.elizabethstreet cafe.com; 1501 S 1st St; pastries $2-7, breakfast $8-19, lunch & dinner $9-23; 8am-10:30pm Sun-Thu, to 11pm Fri & Sat)

Uchi

JAPANESE $$$

22 Map p66, E2

East and West collide beautifully at this top-notch South Austin sushi joint run by owner and executive chef Tyson Cole. The sleek interior would feel right at home in LA, and the sushi is every bit as fresh and imaginative as what you'd get there. (512-916-4808; www.uchiaustin.com; 801 S Lamar Blvd; sushi & small plates $3-22, sushi rolls $10-13; 5-10pm Sun-Thu, to 11pm Fri & Sat)

Drinking

ABGB

BEER GARDEN

23 Map p66, C5

Want a place to meet your friends for beer and conversation? Then settle in at a picnic table inside or out at this convivial brewery and beer garden that's also known for its great food. The boar, tasso and spinach pizza? Oh yes, you do want a slice of this thin-crusted specialty pie ($4). Live music Tuesday and Wednesday, and Friday through Sunday. (Austin Beer Garden Brewery; 512-298-2242; www.theabgb.com; 1305 W Oltorf St; 11:30am-11pm Tue-Thu, 11:30am-midnight Fri, noon-midnight Sat, noon-10pm Sun;)

Hotel San José

BAR

24 Map p66, G4

Transcending the hotel-bar genre, this is actually a cool, Zen-like outdoor patio that attracts a chill crowd, and it's a nice place to hang if you want to actually have a conversation. Service can be leisurely, but maybe that's OK for an oasis? (512-852-2350; 1316 S Congress Ave; noon-midnight)

Understand

Lady Bird Lake: What's Your Name, Again?

What's the name of the body of water dividing downtown from South Austin? Well, it might depend on who you're asking. The lake is a reservoir along the Colorado River, and was formed after the completion of Longhorn Dam in 1960. For decades the lake was known simply as Town Lake. This changed in 2007 after the Austin city council renamed it Lady Bird Lake in honor of the former first lady, who was behind lakeside beautification efforts. The trail around the park was then dubbed Lady Bird Lake Trail. That name was changed to the Ann & Roy Butler Hike-and-Bike Trail in 2011 to honor former mayor Roy Butler and his wife Ann. To add to the confusion, the Colorado River reservoir below Mount Bonnell northwest of downtown is known as Lake Austin. Got it? No worries if you don't – you'll hear all of these various names, and no one will fuss with you if you get it wrong.

Jo's Coffee
TEX-MEX, SANDWICHES $

Walk-up window, friendly staff, shaded patio, plus great people-watching... Throw in breakfast tacos, gourmet deli sandwiches and coffee drinks. Stick it in the middle of hopping South Congress (see 4 ☉ Map p66, G3), and you've got a classic Austin hangout. Don't miss the *I Love You So Much* mural (p68) on the north side. (☎512-444-3800; www.joscoffee.com; 1300 S Congress Ave; tacos $3.50, sandwiches $6-9; ☉7am-9pm; ☎)

Entertainment

Broken Spoke
LIVE MUSIC

25 ☆ ◉ Map p66, A5

George Strait once hung from the wagon-wheel chandeliers at the wooden-floored Broken Spoke, a true Texas honky-tonk. Not sure of your dance moves? Take a lesson. They're offered from 8pm to 9pm Wednesday through Saturday. As the sign inside says: 'Please do Not!!!! Stand on the Dance Floor.' (www.brokenspokeaustintx. net; 3201 S Lamar Blvd; ☉11am-11:30pm Tue, to midnight Wed & Thu, to 1:30am Fri & Sat)

Continental Club
LIVE MUSIC

26 ☆ ◉ Map p66, G4

No passive toe-tapping here; this 1950s-era lounge has a dance floor that's always swinging with some of the city's best local acts. On most Monday nights you can catch local legend Dale Watson and his Lone Stars (10:15pm). (☎512-441-2444; www. continentalclub.com; 1315 S Congress Ave; ☉4pm-2am Mon-Sun, from 3pm Sat & Sun)

Alamo Drafthouse Cinema – S Lamar Blvd   CINEMA

27 Map p66, D2

Like the other outposts of this Austin-based movie chain, the focus is on the movie-going experience. Reserved seating. No latecomers to sessions. No talking or texting. Just pure movie enjoyment. Food and alcohol served. (☏512-861-7040; www.drafthouse.com; 1120 S Lamar Blvd; movies $10.75-14.75)

Long Center for the Performing Arts   PERFORMING ARTS

28 Map p66, F2

This state-of-the-art theater opened in late 2008 as part of a waterfront redevelopment along Lady Bird Lake. The multistage venue hosts drama, dance, concerts and comedians. Also known for its gorgeous view of the downtown skyline from its outdoor terrace. (☏512-457-5100; www.thelongcenter.org; 701 W Riverside Dr)

Saxon Pub   LIVE MUSIC

29 Map p66, D3

The super-chill Saxon Pub, presided over by 'Rusty,' a huge knight who sits out the front, has music every night, mostly Texas performers in the blues-rock vein. A great place to kick back, drink a beer and discover a new favorite artist. (☏512-448-2552; www.thesaxonpub.com; 1320 S Lamar Blvd)

Emo's East   LIVE MUSIC

30 Map p66, H4

For over 20 years, Emo's led the pack in the punk and indie scene in a crowded space on Red River St. Since 2011, it's been enjoying some shiny new digs (and a whole lot more space) out on Riverside. (☏tickets 888-512-7469; www.emosaustin.com; 2015 E Riverside Dr; ⊙showtimes vary)

Shopping

Austin Art Garage   ART

31 Map p66, B4

This cool little independent...well, we hesitate to call it a 'gallery' because that would needlessly scare some people off. Anyway, it features some pretty great artwork by Austin artists. (Hey, Joel Ganucheau: we're fans.) Check out the website to catch the vibe, and definitely check out the 'gallery' if you like what you see. (☏512-351-5934; www.austinartgarage.com; 2200 S Lamar Blvd; ⊙11am-6pm Tue-Sun)

Lucy in Disguise

VINTAGE

32 🔒 Map p66, G4

Colorful and over the top, this South Congress staple has been outfitting Austinites for years. You can rent or buy costume pieces, which is this place's specialty, but you can also find everyday vintage duds as well. (☑512-444-2002; www.lucyindisguise.com; 1506 S Congress Ave; ◷11am-7pm Mon-Sat, noon-6pm Sun)

Stag

CLOTHING

33 🔒 Map p66, G4

Embrace the art of manliness at this stylish SoCo store that's just for the guys, or for girls who are shopping for guys. (☑512-373-7824; www.stagaustin.com; 1423 S Congress Ave; ◷11am-7pm Mon-Thu, to 8pm Fri & Sat, to 6pm Sun)

Yard Dog

ART

34 🔒 Map p66, F4

Stop into this small but scrappy gallery that focuses on folk and outsider art. (☑512-912-1613; www.yarddog.com; 1510 S Congress Ave; ◷11am-5pm Mon-Fri, 11am-6pm Sat, noon-5pm Sun)

Amelia's Retrovogue & Relics

VINTAGE

35 🔒 Map p66, E5

Austin's queen of vintage high fashion, Amelia's offers *Vogue*-worthy dresses, retro '50s bathing suits and other old-school glamour for both men and women. It's a favorite with film-industry folk. (☑512-442-4446; www.ameliasretrovogue.com; 2213 S 1st St; ◷noon-5pm Tue-Sat)

Blackmail

CLOTHING

36 🔒 Map p66, G3

Black is the new black at this store that unites Goths, punks and urban sophisticates. That means gorgeous black dresses and *guayabera* shirts, black-and-silver jewelry, black beaded handbags, black shoes and even minimalist black-and-white home decor. (☑512-804-5881; 1202 S Congress Ave; ◷11am-7pm Mon-Sat, to 6pm Sun)

Birds Barbershop

COSMETICS

37 🔒 Map p66, C4

Hippest cut in town; buzzcut $15. Complimentary Shiner beer included with cut. (☑512-442-8800; www.birdsbarbershop.com; 2110 S Lamar Blvd; ◷9am-8pm Mon-Fri, to 7pm Sat, 10am-6pm Sun)

Lucy in Disguise

Local Life
Urban Hike: Zilker Park & Barton Creek Greenbelt

Getting There

🚗 Park in the Barton Springs parking lot south of Barton Springs Rd.

🚌 The Greenbelt is served by the 30 bus.

Hundred-year-old Zilker Park is home to an entertaining mix of natural and man-made attractions. Many of the best are easily enjoyed near Barton Springs Pool. At the southwest end of the Barton Springs parking lot, you'll find the eastern trailhead to the 7.5-mile long Barton Creek Greenbelt.

❶ Hit the Water

Lakes, creeks and pools are what make **Zilker Park** (p60) special. To watch folks launching from shore into Barton Creek and paddlers on the water, walk to **Zilker Park Boat Rentals** (p61), which is tucked below the far eastern end of the Barton Springs Pool parking lot, downstream from the pool. This 45-year old company rent canoes, kayaks and stand-up paddleboards.

❷ Family Fun

Just upstream kids enjoy the playground. A few steps away is the ticket office for the family friendly **Zilker Zephyr** (☎512-478-8286; 2201 Barton Springs Rd; adult/child $3/2; ◷10am-5pm). This open-air mini-train makes a 3-mile loop around the park on a 20- to 25-minute run.

❸ Barton Springs Pool

You'll find swimmers and waders enjoying this spring-fed **pool** (☎512-867-3080; 2201 Barton Springs Rd; adult/child $8/3; ◷5am-10pm) year round – about 600,000 annually they say. For a unique animal sighting, keep a lookout for the endangered Barton Springs Salamander. This cold-blooded critter grows to a length of 2½ inches and lives only in the four springs comprising Barton Springs. Plans are afoot – and growing more expensive – to create a 75-foot-long waterway here as a new habitat for the salamander.

❹ Back to Nature

For a longer walk, hook up with the **Barton Creek Greenbelt** (p68). This well-used hiking and biking trail is dotted with swimming holes and limestone cliffs, the latter popular with rock climbers farther along the trail. This is also the start of the Violet Crown Trail, which joins the greenbelt for about 4 miles. On the way to the next trailhead, you'll pass Campbell's Swimming Hole.

❺ Tacos & Trail Hiking

The next greenbelt access point after Zilker Park is 1500 Spyglass Rd, about 1.2 miles southwest of the Barton Springs entrance. This trailhead is actually closer to Campbell's Swimming Hole than Zilker Park. But perhaps the best part about the Spyglass trailhead is its proximity to **Tacodeli** (p71), known for its fast and tasty breakfast tacos. Stock up here. If you continue south on the greenbelt from the Spyglass trailhead, look for rock climbers.

Explore

UT & Central Austin

The University of Texas cuts a huge swath across the city just north of downtown; look for the main tower (pictured above) and you'll know you've arrived. Even if you're not an alum or a UT Longhorn at heart, the campus is a pleasant place to stroll. It's also home to several worthwhile museums, although it's a long walk if you want to cover them all in one visit.

The Sights in a Day

☼ Kickstart your morning with a few homespun stories from the animatronic Lyndon B Johnson at his namesake **library & museum** (p82) on the northeast edge of the UT campus. For a look at Texas flora and fauna – much of it stuffed – walk over to the nearby **Texas Memorial Museum** (p88).

☼ Head off campus for Detroit-style pizza at **Via 313** (p90) then head back to school for a tour of the UT Tower. From there, take your pick of interesting museums: the **Harry Ransom Humanities Research Center** (p85), home to famous written and photographic works, or the **Blanton Museum of Art** (p85), where the temporary exhibits have some fun with the vast collection.

☾ Celebrate your day of learning with Tex Mex and a margarita at **Trudy's Texas Star** (p88) or settle in at **Scholz Garten** (p90) for German-style good cheer. Up for live music? See who's playing at the on-campus **Cactus Cafe** (p90).

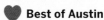

◉ Top Sights

Lyndon Baines Johnson (LBJ) Library & Museum (p82)

University of Texas at Austin (p84)

♥ Best of Austin

Eating
Via 313 (p90)

Drinking
Trudy's Texas Star (p88)

Entertainment
Cactus Cafe (p90)

Getting There

🚲 **Bicycle** There is a B-cycle station at the corner of Congress Ave and E Martin Luther King Jr Blvd.

🚌 **Bus** Bus 1, 10 or 142 from downtown.

Top Sights
Lyndon Baines Johnson (LBJ) Library & Museum

A major renovation brought the museum into the new millennium with interactive exhibits and audiovisual displays. Engaging exhibits trace Johnson's rise to the presidency and focus on his most notable achievements. The man and his story come alive through important artifacts, recordings of his telephone conversations and life-size photos capturing significant or representative moments from his era.

👁 Map p86, C6

📞 512-721-0200

www.lbjlibrary.org

2313 Red River St

adult/child 13-17yr/senior $8/3/5

🕘 9am-5pm

Oval Office replica

Big Personality

The 36th president of the United States was a towering man with a big personality. Visitors can step up beside a life-size photo of the president to get the 'Johnson Treatment' – experiencing what it was like when the tall and imposing president (he was 6ft 3in) leaned close to emphasize a point. Nearby, an animatronic LBJ regales visitors with his recorded stories, highlighting the former president's skill at connecting with voters by emphasizing his homespun Texas roots.

November 22, 1963

Johnson became president of the United States on November 22, 1963, after his predecessor John F Kennedy was assassinated in Dallas. A moving exhibit spotlights events on that tragic day and the days following. One photograph shows Johnson taking the oath of office on Air Force One with his wife Lady Bird on one side and first lady Jacqueline Kennedy on the other. A letter from the first lady to LBJ thanking him for his kindness and support is also shown. You'll also see notes from Johnson's remarks at Andrews Air Force base later that day, his first address to the people as president.

Oval Office

Ride the elevator to the 10th floor to see an exact replica of the Oval Office during Johnson's presidency. Well, almost exact. This one is 7/8ths of the room's actual size. Note the photograph of LBJ's presidential inspiration, Franklin Delano Roosevelt. Roosevelt appointed Johnson to be the Texas director of the National Youth Administration when Johnson was in his twenties. One amusing artifact? Johnson's recorded phone conversation with Katharine Graham, publisher of the *Washington Post*. On this particular call, he lays on the charm pretty darn thick.

☑ **Top Tip**

▶ Parking lot 38 borders the sidewalk leading to the museum. It offers free parking, but the other lots beside it do not. Look for the banners at the entrance and double-check the signage.

✕ **Take a Break**

For lunch, head east from campus to Manor Rd, lined with fantastic restaurants. It's hard to go wrong with a taco from El Chilito (p51).

Top Sights
University of Texas at Austin

Whatever you do, don't call it 'Texas University' – them's fightin' words, usually used derisively by Texas A&M students to take their rivals down a notch. Sorry, A&M, but the main campus of the University of Texas is kind of a big deal. Established in 1883, UT has the largest enrollment in the state, with over 50,000 students.

👁 Map p86, A6

www.utexas.edu

cnr University Ave & 24th St

UT's Littlefield Fountain

Blanton Museum of Art

A big university with a big endowment is bound to have a big art collection, and now, finally, it has a suitable building to show it off properly. With one of the best university art collections in the USA, the **Blanton** (📞512-471-5482; www.blantonmuseum.org; 200 E Martin Luther King Jr Blvd; adult/child $9/free; 10am-5pm Tue-Fri, 11am-5pm Sat, 1-5pm Sun) showcases a variety of styles. It doesn't go very deeply into any of them, but then again you're bound to find something of interest. Especially striking is the permanent installation of Missao/Missoes (How to Build Cathedrals) – which involves 600,000 pennies, 800 communion wafers and 2000 cattle bones.

Harry Ransom Humanities Research Center

The fascinating **Ransom Center** (📞512-471-8944; www.hrc.utexas.edu; 300 W 21st St; admission free; 10am-5pm Mon-Wed & Fri, to 7pm Thu, noon-5pm Sat & Sun) is a major repository of historic manuscripts, photography, books, film, TV, music and more. Highlights include a complete copy of the Gutenberg Bible (one of only five in the USA) and what is thought to be the first photograph ever taken, from 1826. Check the website for special online-only exhibitions and the center's busy events calendar of author readings, live music, lectures and more.

UT Tower

No building defines the UT campus as much as the UT Tower. Standing 307ft high, with a clock over 12ft in diameter, the tower looms large, both as a campus landmark and in Austin history as the perch used during a 1966 shooting spree. On a more cheerful note, it now serves as a beacon of victory when it's lit orange to celebrate a Longhorn win or other achievement. The tower's observation deck is accessible only by **guided tours** (📞512-475-6636; http://tower.utexas.edu; $6; hours vary seasonally).

☑ Top Tips

▶ Want to see some Big 12 football or other college athletics while you're in town? The **UT Box Office** (📞512-471-3333; www.texassports.com; 2139 San Jacinto Blvd, Darrel K Royal-Texas Memorial Stadium) is your source for all things Longhorn.

▶ Admission is free on Thursdays at the Blanton Museum.

✖ Take a Break

The patio is the place to be for a coffee or beer at Spider House (p90).

Or, kick back with bratwurst and a beer in the festive Scholz Garten (p90).

Interregional Hwy

Red River St
Caswell Ave
Bennett Ave
E 47th St
E 46th St
E 45th St
Caswell Ave
Park Blvd
E 41st St
E 38th 1/2 St
E 38th St
Duval St
Elisabet Ney Museum

HYDE PARK

Barrow Ave
E 41st St

HANCOCK

Avenue F
E 45th St
E 44th St
Red River St
Peck Ave

Avenue F
W 45th St
E 43rd St
Avenue D
Avenue H
Duval St
Texas Ave
Carolyn Ave
Harris Ave

Avenue C
W 43rd St
W 42nd St
Speedway
E 41st St
E 40th St
Avenue G
E 38th St
Duval St
E 35th St

W 44th St
Avenue B
Avenue A
W 41st St
W 40th St
W 39th St
E 34th St
E 33rd St
E 32nd St

Guadalupe St
W 38th 1/2 St
Speedway
Helms St
E 31st St

W 37th St
W 35th St
W 34th St
University Ave

W 35th St
W 34th St
W 33rd St
CENTRAL AUSTIN
W 30th St
Adams Park
W 29th St

King St
W 32nd St
Guadalupe St

W 38th St
W 34th St
W 32nd St
W 30th St

500 m
0.25 miles

A 1 B 1 C 1 D 1 E 1
A 2 B 2
A 3 B 3
A 4 B 4

CHERRYWOOD

Werner Ave
Hollywood Ave
Robinson Ave
Edgewood Ave

Coledo St
Alamo St
Alamo Pocket Park
Chicon St
Poquito St
E 22nd St

Breeze Tce
French Pl
Lafayette Ave
Dancy St
E 29th St
E 28th St
E 31st St
E 30th St

Manor Rd
E 20th St
E Martin Luther King Jr Blvd
E 18th St

EAST AUSTIN

E 16th St

Duncan La
E 32nd St

E Dean Keeton St

Leona St

Mount Calvary Cemetery

Comal St

Oakwood Cemetery

Red River St
Red River St

HANCOCK
Medical Arts St

Interregional Hwy

Lyndon Baines Johnson (LBJ) Library & Museum

Clyde Littlefield Dr

E 32nd St
Bellevue Pl
Harris Park Ave
Eastwoods Neighbourhood Park

Trinity St

Robert Dedman Dr

E 30th St
Speedway

University of Texas at Austin

E Dean Keeton St

Texas Memorial 3 Museum

E 23rd St

San Jacinto Blvd

East Mall

Waller Creek

E 21st St

Speedway

E Martin Luther King Jr Blvd

Red River St
Waterloo Park

Trinity St

12

W 27th St

Whitis

University of Texas at Austin

W Dean Keeton St

11

University of Texas at Austin

West Mall

15

1 Hi, How Are You Mural

Inner Campus Cir

W 24th St
W 22nd St
W 21st St

W 20th St
University Ave

W Martin Luther King Jr Blvd

E Martin Luther King Jr Blvd
E 18th St
E 17th St

N Congress Ave

10

Nueces St
Guadalupe St
Speedway

Guadalupe St
Lavaca St

W 18th St
W 17th St
W 16th St
N 16th St

DOWNTOWN

Megabus

Sights

Hi, How Are You Mural   PUBLIC ART

1 ⊙ Map p86, A7

Created by songwriter and artist Daniel Johnston, this bug-eyed frog greets passersby near the University of Texas. The mural, also known as *Jeremiah the Innocent,* covers the south wall of a Thai restaurant known as Thai, How Are You – which changed its name from the less punny Thai Spice. (21st St & Guadalupe)

Elisabet Ney Museum   MUSEUM

2 ⊙ Map p86, D1

A German-born sculptor and spirited trailblazer, Elisabet Ney lived in Austin in the early 1880s, and her former studio is now one of the oldest museums in Texas. Filled with more than 100 works of art, including busts and statues of political figures, the castlelike building made from rough-hewn stone is reason enough to visit.

Look for the hidden door on the 2nd floor. (☎512-974-1625; www.austintexas.gov/department/elisabet-ney-museum; 304 E 44th St; donations welcome; ⊙noon-5pm Wed-Sun)

Texas Memorial Museum   MUSEUM

3 ⊙ Map p86, C6

We all know how kids feel about dinosaurs, and this natural history museum is the perfect place for them to indulge their fascination. Look up to see the swooping skeleton of the Texas Pterosaur – one of the most famous dino finds ever. This impressively humongous Cretaceous-era flying reptile has a wingspan of 40ft and was recovered at Big Bend in 1971. There are other exhibits, too, focusing on anthropology, natural history, geology and biodiversity. (☎512-471-1604; www.tmm.utexas.edu; 2400 Trinity St; adult/child $4/3; ⊙9am-5pm Tue-Sat; 👪)

Eating

Trudy's Texas Star   TEX-MEX $

4 ✕ Map p86, A4

Get your Tex-Mex fix here; the menu is consistently good, with several healthier-than-usual options. But we'll let you in on a little secret: this place could serve nothing but beans and dirt and people would still line up for the margaritas, which might very well be the best in Austin. (☎512-477-2935; www.trudys.com; 409

Local Life
Student Life

Want to immerse in college culture? Then go where the students go. Step into the University Co-op (p91) for Longhorn mementos then stroll busy Guadalupe St, aka The Drag, on the western edge of the school. Interact with student guides on the UT Tower Tours (p85).

GIULIA M/SHUTTERSTOCK ©

Tex-Mex burritos

W 30th St; breakfast $6-11, lunch & dinner $8-19; ⊙11am-2am Mon-Fri, from 9am Sat & Sun)

New World Deli

SANDWICHES $

5 🍴 Map p86, B2

Fans of the sandwich will be delighted with the offerings at New World, whether they're after a sloppy joe, pastrami on rye, or curried chicken salad on wheat – all of which are made with New World's amazing, fresh-baked bread, and all of which will raise the bar on what you'll expect from any future sandwiches you encounter. (☏512-451-7170; www. newworlddeli.com; 4101 Guadalupe St;

sandwiches $6-9; ⊙11am-9pm Mon-Sat, to 5pm Sun)

Freebirds World Burrito

MEXICAN $

6 🍴 Map p86, E3

Burritos – and nothing but – are why you come to Freebirds. Each one is custom-made under your watchful eye, with a boggling number of combinations of tortilla, meat and toppings. For a place with kind of a rock-and-roll atmosphere, the staff is surprisingly friendly and helpful. (☏512-451-5514; www.freebirds.com; 1000 E 41st St; burritos under $10; ⊙10:30am-10pm Mon-Sat, to 9pm Sun)

Via 313
PIZZA $$

7 Map p86, A4

What? Why is my pizza a square? Because it's Detroit-style, baby, meaning it's cooked in a square pan, plus there's caramelized cheese on the crust and sauce layered over the toppings. And after just one bite of one of these rich favorites, we guarantee you'll forget all geometric concerns. Good craft beer selection too. (☎512-358-6193; www.via313.com; 3016 Guadalupe St; pizzas $10-29; ⏱11am-11pm Sun-Thu, to 11pm Fri & Sat)

Hyde Park Bar & Grill
AMERICAN $$

8 Map p86, D2

Look for the enormous fork out front to guide you to this homey neighborhood haunt. The diverse menu has plenty of options, but no matter what you choose, we insist that you order the batter-dipped French fries, which is what this place is famous for. (☎512-458-3168; www.hpbng.com; 4206 Duval St; mains $8-19; ⏱11am-10:30pm Mon-Thu, to 11pm Fri & Sat, 10:30am-10:30pm Sun)

Q **Local Life**
Coffee & Wi-fi

If you want to chill out over coffee in a low-key and student-friendly setting, head to the eclectic Spider House (p90), where the table-filled patio is a great spot for lounging and using the wi-fi. Serves craft beer and cocktails too.

Drinking

Spider House
CAFE

9 Map p86, A4

Traveling carnival? Haunted house? Or a European cafe with a great patio? North of campus, Spider House has a big, funky outdoor area bedecked with all sorts of oddities. It's open late and also serves beer and wine. In the afternoon, bring a laptop, sip coffee and use the wi-fi, available until 2am. (☎512-480-9562; 2908 Fruth St; ⏱11am-2am; 🛜)

Scholz Garten
BEER HALL

10 Map p86, B8

This German *biergarten* has been around forever – or at least since 1866 – and its proximity to the capitol building has made it the traditional favorite of politicians. The author O Henry was also a fan. (☎512-474-1958; 1607 San Jacinto Blvd; ⏱11am-11pm)

Entertainment

Cactus Cafe
LIVE MUSIC

11 Map p86, A6

Listen to acoustic up close and personal at this intimate club on the UT campus. (www.cactuscafe.org; Texas Union, cnr 24th & Guadalupe Sts; ⏱showtimes vary)

Frank Erwin Center
STADIUM

12 Map p86, C8

This arena hosts big-name concerts, UT men's and women's basketball

Understand

Civil Rights & Social Justice

Johnson spearheaded much of the social justice legislation passed in the 1960s, all part of his vision for a Great Society that would provide 'liberty and abundance for all.' The results of his efforts to reduce poverty, improve education and secure Civil Rights for all Americans live on today through the many programs he supported. The Social Justice Gallery in the Lyndon Baines Johnson (LBJ) Library & Museum (p82) discusses these different projects and programs, from civil rights to Medicare to public broadcasting and consumer protection. The Civil Rights exhibit displays the desk on which Johnson signed the Civil Rights Act of 1965.

games, and graduation ceremonies. (512-471-7744; www.uterwinecenter.com; 1701 Red River St)

Hyde Park Theatre THEATER

13 Map p86, B1

This is one of Austin's coolest small theaters, presenting regional premieres of off-Broadway hits and recent Obie (Off-Broadway Theater Awards) winners. Its annual FronteraFest presents more than 100 new works over five weeks at venues around town. (512-479-7529; www.fronterafest.org; 511 W 43rd St)

Shopping

Antone's Records MUSIC

14 Map p86, A4

North of UT, legendary Antone's was founded in 1972 and has a well-respected selection of Austin, Texas and American blues music (with plenty of rare vinyl), plus a bulletin board for musicians, and vintage concert posters for sale. (512-322-0660; www.antonesrecordshop.com; 2928 Guadalupe St; 10am-10pm Mon-Sat, 11am-8pm Sun)

University Co-op GIFTS & SOUVENIRS

15 Map p86, A6

Stock up on souvenirs sporting the Longhorn logo at this store brimming with spirit. It's amazing the quantity of objects that come in burnt orange and white. (512-476-7211; www.universitycoop.com; 2246 Guadalupe St; 9am-8pm Mon-Fri, to 7pm Sat, 10am-6pm Sun)

Buffalo Exchange CLOTHING

16 Map p86, A4

The Austin branch of this nationwide used-clothing chain has an impressive selection of vintage clothes and shoes for men and women, including Texas styles and Western wear. (512-480-9922; 2904 Guadalupe St; 10am-9pm Mon-Sat, 11am-8pm Sun)

Explore

Market District, Clarksville & North Austin

West of downtown, the Market District draws shoppers to its large natural foods market and several iconic stores. An eye-catching graffiti wall shares the colorful visions of spray-paint artists. Compact Clarksville is one of the city's oldest neighborhoods. North Austin is largely residential but a few fantastic restaurants and bars add pizzazz. Just north of campus, Hyde Park was Austin's first suburb.

The Sights in a Day

For those about to shop, we salute you. This day starts with juice and a snack from the flagship **Whole Foods Market** (pictured left; p99) – the famous natural foods market started in Austin. From here, stroll across the street to flip through the vinyl at **Waterloo Records** (p95) followed by an hour or two browsing the stacks at **Book People** (p95).

Grab a hearty lunch at **Kerbey Lane Café** (p99) with a scoop of ice cream from **Amy's Ice Creams** (p98) for dessert. Then check out the wild spray-paint art at the **Hope Outdoor Gallery** (p98). For vintage finds, head to North Austin.

Soak up the sounds of Johnny Cash at the **Mean Eyed Cat** (p102) then mosey over to **Ginny's Little Longhorn Saloon** (p101) for live music. From 5pm to 6pm Monday through Saturday, Lone Star drafts are $1! On Sunday, definitely stop by at 4pm for chicken-shit bingo.

For a local's day in the Market District, see p94.

Local Life
Market Stroll (p94)

Best of Austin

Eating
Uchiko (p98)

Kerbey Lane Café (p99)

Barley Swine (p100)

Drinking
Mean Eyed Cat (p102)

Ginny's Little Longhorn Saloon (p101)

Getting There

Bike There is a B-Cycle station at W 5th St and Bowie St beside Whole Foods Market.

Bus From downtown, bus 4, 21 and others will get you to the Market District. Bus 338 runs along Lamar Blvd, north and south of Lady Bird Lake.

Car The main road is N Lamar Ave, which runs north–south through the neighborhood, eventually crossing Lady Bird Lake into South Austin. The western border is MoPac Expy/Hwy Loop 1.

Local Life
Market Stroll

Anchored by Whole Foods Market, the traffic-heavy Market District is a great spot for concentrated shopping, especially if you don't like malls. There's dedicated parking for the larger shops, and the market has become a social hub of sorts, with a wide selection of eateries inside and a lively patio beside the front parking lot.

1 Whole Day...in the Market

Open since 1980, this colossal **Whole Foods** (p99) is the flagship store for the nation-wide natural foods grocery chain. It's a bit of a zoo, but that's part of the fun. The craziness starts in the underground parking garage, where you might encounter an employee directing traffic. Inside are stations for tacos, sushi, coffee and more. On weekends, there's live music on the patio.

❷ Records Ain't Retro

Across W 6th St is beloved **Waterloo Records** (☎512-474-2500; www.waterloorecords.com; 600 N Lamar Blvd; ⏱10am-11pm Mon-Sat, from 11am Sun), which opened in 1982. The store is spacious and well-stocked. Come here to buy or sell new and used vinyl, CDs and DVDs. Texas artists are well represented in the inventory. Look for in-store performances. The best part may be the helpful and welcoming service – no old-school record-store snobs here.

❸ Gear Up for the Outdoors

To buy last-minute hiking and backpacking equipment before heading out to Big Bend National Park, step inside **REI** (601 N Lamar Blvd; www.rei.com) across the street from Waterloo. It also sells clothing, footwear, and books and maps.

❹ Bookworm Paradise

If you're into books, **Book People** (☎512-472-5050; 603 N Lamar Blvd; ⏱9am-11pm) feels like an old friend. As you wander the stacks, you'll notice detailed staff recommendations beneath the packed-tight shelves. There's a strong travel section in back. The store holds more than 300 book signings per year, so there's likely somebody of interest in-house on any given week. If you've got younger kids, stop by for story time at 11:30am on Saturdays. Take a break at the cafe, which serves coffee, sandwiches and desserts.

❺ Walk in the Park

For a brief communion with nature, pause by Shoal Creek in **Duncan Park**.

❻ Graffiti Works

If it's not too hot and you don't mind a half-mile walk one-way, you can see a mesmerizing hotspot for wall art. Covering multi-level concrete ruins just off of N Lamar Blvd, **Graffiti Hill** is a showcase for local graffiti artists, who have spray-painted the walls here with an impressive array of styles and designs. The non-profit **Hope Outdoor Gallery** (p98) manages the site, and artists must secure a permit. Proceeds from gallery events support education.

See North Austin Inset (1.6mi)

Sights

Hope Outdoor Gallery GALLERY

1 Map p96, F2

For a wild collision of colors and art, make your way to this sprawling collection of graffiti that's been spray-painted across multilevel concrete ruins. The on-site open-air gallery here is run by the HOPE Foundation, a collection of creatives who support education. To add your own art, email murals@hopecampaign.org for a permit. Note that the property could be closed or repurposed at any time, so get there now. (Grafitti Park at Castle Hill; http://hopecampaign.org; 11th St & Baylor St; ⏱9am-7pm)

Castle Hill Fitness GYM

2 Map p96, G2

The focus here is on classes and fitness machines. Check out the website for information on super-affordable two-week memberships or 10-visit passes. (☎512-478-4567; www.

Top Tip

Neighborhood Dining

If you just stick to the buzziest restaurants, you'll miss some fantastic neighborhood standbys, from the hearty breakfasts at Kerbey Lane Café to the beloved Mexican dishes at Fonda San Miguel (p101), to the dinners at night-out favorite Wink (p101).

castlehillfitness.com; 1112 N Lamar Blvd; ⏱5:30am-10pm Mon-Thu, to 9pm Fri, 8am-7pm Sat & Sun)

Eating

Amy's Ice Creams ICE CREAM $

3 Map p96, F4

It's not just the ice cream we love; it's the toppings that get pounded and blended in, violently but lovingly, by the staff wielding a metal scoop in each hand. Look for other locations on Guadalupe St north of the UT campus, on South Congress near all the shops, or at the airport for a last-ditch fix. (☎512-480-0673; www.amysicecreams.com; 1012 W 6th St; ice cream $3.25-6; ⏱11:30am-midnight Sun-Thu, to 1am Fri & Sat)

Uchiko JAPANESE $$$

4 Map p96, B5

Not content to rest on his Uchi laurels, chef Tyson Cole opened this North Lamar restaurant that describes itself as 'Japanese farmhouse dining.' But we're here to tell you, it's hard to imagine being treated to fantastic and unique delicacies such as these and enjoying this sort of bustling ambience in any Japanese farmhouse. Reservations are highly recommended. (☎512-916-4808; www.uchikoaustin.com; 4200 N Lamar Blvd; small plates $4-28, sushi rolls $10-16; ⏱5-10pm Sun-Thu, to 11pm Fri & Sat)

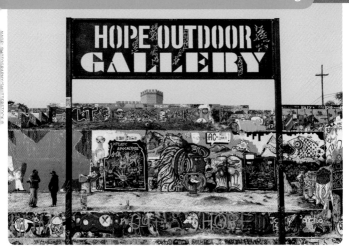

Hope Outdoor Gallery

Whole Foods Market

MARKET $

5 Map p96, F4

The flagship of the Austin-founded Whole Foods Market is a gourmet grocery and cafe with restaurant counters and a staggering takeaway buffet, including self-made salads, global mains, deli sandwiches and more. The sushi tuna burritos ($11) from the sushi counter are particularly delicious.

If there's no parking in the lot out front, head to the free underground garage. (www.wholefoods.com; 525 N Lamar Blvd; sandwiches $6-9, mains $6-15; ⊙7am-10pm; 🛜)

Kerbey Lane Café

AMERICAN $

6 Map p96, A5

Kerbey Lane is a longtime Austin favorite, fulfilling round-the-clock cravings for anything from ginger-bread pancakes to black-bean tacos to mahimahi. Try the addictive Kerbey Queso while you wait. (They have vegan queso, too!) There are several other locations around town, but this location in a homey bungalow is the original and has the most character. (☎512-451-1436; www.kerbeylanecafe.com; 3704 Kerbey Lane; breakfast $6-13, lunch & dinner $9-13; ⊙6:30am-11pm Mon-Thu, 24hr from 6:30am Fri–11pm Sun; 🖋 👶)

CHRISTIAN SCIENCE MONITOR/GETTY IMAGES ©

Country music and dancing at Ginny's Little Longhorn Saloon

Stiles Switch BARBECUE $

7 Map p96, B4

With manageable lines, you won't have to suffer to enjoy outstanding brisket, fired up to tender, smoky perfection, at this popular eatery 6 miles north of downtown. Top it off with some ribs, a side of corn casserole and a local microbrew. (☏512-380-9199; www.stilesswitchbbq.com; 6610 N Lamar Blvd; mains $7-18; ☺11am-9pm Tue-Thu, to 10pm Fri & Sat, to 9pm Sun)

Hut's Hamburgers BURGERS $

8 Map p96, G5

Choose from natural grass-fed cattle, buffalo meat or chicken for your burger at this Austin roadhouse (it

opened in 1939). Southern mains, like chicken-fried steak, are pretty good too. A vegan veggie burger is also available. (☏512-472-0693; www.hutsfrank andangies.com; 807 W 6th St; meals $6-11; ☺11am-9:30pm Sun-Tue, to 10pm Wed-Sat)

Barley Swine AMERICAN $$$

9 Map p96, B4

Small plates. Tantalizing flavors. Locally sourced. Changing menus. Snout-to-tail culinary creations. And craft cocktails. All served in a rustically chic setting. Yep, hardcore farm-to-table joints are trending these days, but Barley Swine has a sense of fun often missing from similar establishments. Why yes, I will have the Rotating Obligatory Tiki – only $6 during the

Swine Time happy hour (4pm to 7pm Monday to Friday). (📞512-394-8150; www.barleyswine.com; 6555 Burnet Rd; small plates $9-30; ⏱5-10pm Sun-Thu, to 11pm Fri & Sat)

Wink FUSION $$$

 10 Map p96, G2

Date night? At this intimate gem hidden behind Whole Earth Provision Co, diners are ushered to tables underneath windows screened with Japanese rice paper, then presented with an exceptional wine list. The chef-inspired fare takes on a nouveau fusion attitude that is equal parts modern French and Asian. For a special splurge, try the five-course ($68) tasting menu. (📞512-482-8868; 1014 N Lamar Blvd; mains $17-33; ⏱6-9:30pm Mon-Wed, 5:30-9:30pm Thu-Sat)

Fonda San Miguel MEXICAN $$$

 11 Map p96, A4

The gorgeous building is drenched in the atmosphere of old Mexico, with folk-inspired art, and it's been serving interior Mexican cooking for over 25 years. The Sunday brunch buffet is an impressive event but, at $39 per person, you'd better come hungry to make it worthwhile. Note that the last seating is one hour before close. (📞512-459-4121; 2330 W North Loop Blvd; mains $16-39; ⏱5:30-9:30pm Mon-Thu, to 10:30pm Fri & Sat, 11am-2pm Sun)

Local Life

Uchiko Sake Social

Stylish Uchiko (p98) is lauded by locals for its fresh and exquisitely flavored sushi and seafood dishes. But prices are steep, reflecting the high quality of the fare. On a budget? Don't despair, just come to eat early. To sample the food at wallet- and purse-friendly prices, visit during the **Sake Social** happy hour, held nightly from 5pm to 6:30pm. Several rolls are $6, while a half-dozen small bites under $7 offer a broad sampling of the delectable Japanese menu. Sake, beer and wine selections range from $3 to $7.

Drinking

Ginny's Little Longhorn Saloon BAR

12 Map p96, A4

This funky little cinder-block building is one of those dive bars that Austinites love so very much – and did even before it became nationally famous for chicken-shit bingo on Sunday night. The place gets so crowded during bingo that you can barely see the darn chicken – but, hey, it's still fun. The overflow crowd is out back. (📞512-524-1291; www.thelittlelonghorn saloon.com; 5434 Burnet Rd; ⏱5pm-midnight Tue & Wed, to 1am Thu-Sat, 2-10pm Sun)

> ### Understand
> #### I Scream You Scream
> ─────────────
>
> Short of jumping into Barton Springs, there's no better way to cool off than at Amy's Ice Creams (p98). It's not just the ice cream itself, which, by the way, is smooth, creamy and delightful. It's the toppings – pardon us, *crush'ns* they call 'em – that get pounded and blended in, violently but lovingly, by staff wielding a metal scoop in each hand. Mexican vanilla bean with fresh strawberries, dark chocolate with Reese's Peanut Butter Cups, or mango with jelly beans if that's what you're into. With 15 flavors (rotated from their 300 recipes) and dozens of toppings, ranging from cookies and candy, to fruit or nuts, the combinations aren't endless, but they number too high to count. Look for other locations on Guadalupe St north of the UT campus, on South Congress near all the shops, or at the airport for a last-ditch fix.

Mean Eyed Cat BAR

13 Map p96, B3

We're not sure if this watering hole is a legit dive bar or a calculated dive bar (it opened in 2004). Either way, a bar dedicated to Johnny Cash has our utmost respect. Inside, Man in Black album covers, show posters and other knickknackery adorn the walls of this former chainsaw repair shop. A 300-year-old live oak anchors the lively patio. (☏512-920-6645; www.themeaneyedcat.com; 1621 W 5th St; ⊘11am-2am)

Entertainment

Donn's Depot LIVE MUSIC

14 ⭐ Map p96, C3

Austin loves a dive bar, and Donn's combines a retro atmosphere inside an old railway car with live music six nights a week, including Donn himself performing alongside the Station Masters. A mix of young and old come to Donn's, and the dance floor sees plenty of action. (☏512-478-0336; www.donnsdepot.com; 1600 W 5th St; ⊘2pm-2am Mon-Fri, from 6pm Sat)

Shopping

Blue Velvet VINTAGE

15 Map p96, B4

Western wear, vintage T-shirts and even oddities such as all-American bowling wear hang on the racks at Blue Velvet, where you'll find an equal number of men and women eyeing the goods. Summer fashions are stocked year-round. (☏512-452-2583; www.bluevelvetaustin.com; 217 W North Loop Blvd; ⊘11am-8pm Mon-Sat, to 7pm Sun)

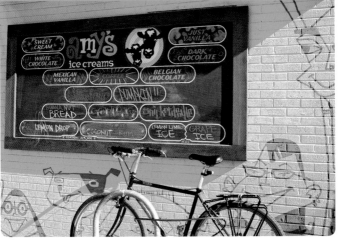

Amy's Ice Creams (p98)

New Bohemia JEWELRY

16 Map p96, C5

When it comes to retro thrift shops, New Bohemia is the place to look for vintage jewelry and clothing. (☎512-326-1238; www.facebook.com/NewBohemia ATX; 4631 Airport Blvd; ☺noon-9pm)

Domain MALL

17 Map p96, A1

Stores like Apple, Neiman Marcus and Anthropologie line the streets of this upscale outdoor shopping center in far northwest Austin. (☎512-795-4230; www.simon.com/mall/the-domain; 11410 Century Oaks Tce; ☺10am-9pm Mon-Sat, noon-6pm Sun)

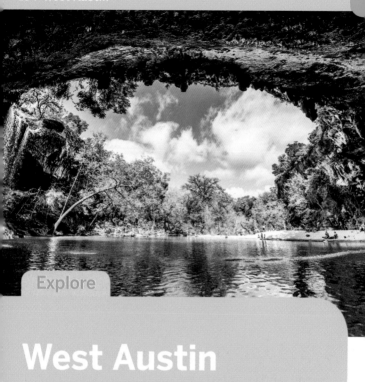

Explore

West Austin

For outdoor recreation beyond Lady Bird Lake, plus a few scenic places to relax and enjoy the afternoon, head west. Parks along Lake Austin draw hikers and nature lovers, while Hamilton Pool Preserve is a gorgeous spot for a refreshing dip. Dripping Springs is the gateway to the Hill Country and keeps Austin day-trippers happy with wineries, microbreweries, distilleries and great restaurants.

The Sights in a Day

☀ Rise and shine with a short climb to the summit of **Mount Bonnell** (p106) and its view of Lake Austin. From here stroll the leafy grounds of the **Mayfield House & Nature Preserve** (p112).

☀ Head west to Dripping Springs for delicious pizza at **Pieous** (p113). From here, take your pick of afternoon libations: craft beer at **Jester King** (p114), spirits at **Treaty Oaks Distilling** (p115) or wine at **Hawk's Shadow Winery** (p115). Not up for drinking? Take a dip in pretty **Hamilton Pool Preserve** (pictured left; p112) – make a reservation before you go in summer.

☾ Explore tiny but intriguing downtown Dripping Springs then settle in for gourmet downhome cookin' – it's a thing – at **Homespun** (p109). After dinner walk to **Mercer Street Dance Hall** (p109) for two-stepping and live music.

For a local's day in Dripping Springs, see p108.

👁 Top Sights
Mount Bonnell (p106)

◯ Local Life
Dripping Springs Walking Tour: Small Town Exploring (p108)

♥ Best of Austin

Eating
Salt Lick (p113)

Pieous (p113)

Drinking
Jester King Brewery (p114)

Treaty Oak Distilling (p115)

Outdoors
Hamilton Pool Preserve (p112)

Getting There

🚗 **Car** To get to Mount Bonnell, follow W 35th St west to Mount Bonnell Rd. To drive to Dripping Springs, follow Hwy 290 W.

Top Sights
Mount Bonnell

On weekends you might find yourself tip-toeing around a wedding ceremony atop Mount Bonnell, the highest point in the city at 775ft. This pretty overlook has impressed day-trippers since the 19th century. At sunset, climb the short but steep stairway for broad views of Lake Austin, the homes along the nearby hillsides and the Hill Country.

◉ Map p110, E1

☎512-974-6700

www.austintexas.gov

3800 Mt Bonnell Rd, Covert Park

History of the Hill

The first recorded mention of Mount Bonnell appeared in 1839 when Albert Sidney Johnson, the Secretary of War for the Republic of Texas, mentioned it in correspondence. Johnson was there to defend the new capital of Austin, and this high viewpoint overlooking the Colorado River was critical for military defense purposes. In subsequent years, as the threat of Native American and Mexican attacks subsided, Mount Bonnell became a favorite spot for sightseers. Maj Gen George Custer picnicked atop Mount Bonnell with his wife Elizabeth after the Civil War. In her book *Tenting on the Plains* she remarked upon the fine views and the steepness of the climb.

Just the Facts

Mount Bonnell is located within Covert Park. The climb from the parking lot to the top of the peak is 102 steps. There's a view deck at the summit, plus a historic marker, but don't stop here. Follow the short trails north and south for a variety of views – and the perfect picnic spot. Lake Austin, visible below, was created after the completion of the Tom Miller Dam in 1940 on the Colorado River.

What's in a Name?

According to the historic marker, Mount Bonnell was named for George Bonnell, a commissioner of Indian Affairs for the Texas Republic. The West Point Society, however, has long believed that the peak was named for Joseph Bonnell, a West Point graduate and Texas military hero. The Society filed a suit with the Court of Appeals in Austin arguing that the Texas State Historical Survey Commission erred when it decided in 1969 that the peak had been named – back in the 1800s – for George Bonnell. The court decided it was a matter best left to the executive branch or the legislature.

☑ Top Tip

▶ No parking in the lot at the base of Mt Bonnell from 10pm to 5am.

✕ Take a Break

Fuel up with a hearty Tex Mex breakfast at Magnolia Cafe (p114).

After a late-morning climb to the summit, drive west to Dripping Springs for pizza and craft beer at Jester King Brewery (p114).

Local Life
Dripping Springs Walking Tour: Small Town Exploring

A small historic district sits along Mercer St in the center of sprawling Dripping Springs, a rural bedroom community about 25 miles west of Austin. The area is known for its outdoor attractions as well as its wineries, crafts breweries and distilleries, but if you don't feel like driving, downtown is an easy and welcoming place to explore by foot, and is especially fun from late afternoon into evening.

1 Coffee with a Smile

You won't find snobby baristas at the ranch-style **Mazama Coffee Co** (☏512-200-6472; www.mazamacoffee.com; 301 Mercer St; ⏲6:30am-6pm Mon-Fri, 8am-5pm Sat, 8am-1pm Sun; 📶) in the morning, just on-the-ball employees who manage to chitchat while keeping the long line moving efficiently. Be sure to order a breakfast taco – if there are any left. In the afternoon, the sunny patio is a nice place to read, meet a friend or

work on your laptop while sipping the house-roasted coffee.

❷ Antiques & Indie Shops

A few doors down, step into **Lone Star Gifts** (☎512-858-9912; www.lonestargifts. net; 301 Mercer St) for an eclectic array of antiques and collectibles from more than 60 vendors. For essential oils, teas and organic herbs visit **Sacred Moon Herbs** (305 Mercer St; www.sacred-moonherbs.com) next door.

❸ No Haircuts Here

Every country town needs at least one hipster bar filled with millennials... right? We jest, but you'll likely spot several microbrew-sipping twenty-somethings in the **Barber Shop** (☎512-829-4636; www.barbershopbar.com; 207 Mercer St; ◷3-11pm Mon-Sat, 2-8pm Sun). If you squint you might just see some Gen-Xers and maybe even a baby boomer sitting around the dark edges of the room. And all are doing just fine at this one-time barber shop. The building, which also did time as a garage, dates to 1924.

❹ Eating at a Friend's House

There's something about **Homespun** (☎512-829-4064; www.homespunkitchen andbar.com; 131 E Mercer St; lunch mains $12-17, dinner mains $17-45; ◷11am-9pm Tue-Thu, to 10pm Fri & Sat, 10am-8pm Sun) that makes you feel like you're chowing down at the cozy home of a good friend – one who also happens to be a fantastic Southern cook. How cozy? You might bump against the band on the front patio as you walk inside. The dining room is a festive place where the chatty owner might just tell you what's tasting good that evening. What's always good? The comfort food mainstays like shrimp and grits, burgers and skillet mac-n-cheese.

❺ Dance On

A bad mood dissolves the moment you step into **Mercer Street Dance Hall** (☎512-858-4314; www.mercerstreet dancehall.com; 332 Mercer St; tickets $7-15, free on Thu; ◷6-11pm Thu, 7pm-midnight Fri, 7pm-1am Sat), where skilled dancers, ice cold beers and a welcoming communal spirit are always on the line-up. Open since 2013, this is one of the region's newest dance halls, but it's embraced the traditions of the classic Texas dance halls in full force, with dance lessons on Saturday nights and top regional acts performing on stage. There are no rules, but standing still on the dance floor just ain't right.

E

Clearview Dr

TARRYTOWN

Mountain View Rd

Mt Bonnell
(2.5mi)

Exposition Blvd

4

Enfield Rd

Quarry Rd

W 12th St

Norwalk La

Norwalk La

D

Dillman St

Cherry La

Bridle Path

Hopi Trail

Pecos St

Bonnie Rd

Exposition Blvd

W 10th St

WESTFIELD

Lions
Municipal
Golf Course

Schulle Ave

Robinhood Trail

Enfield Rd

Raleigh Ave

C

Lake Austin Blvd

Jasper

Lufkin

Lake Austin Blvd

Nocona

Memphis

Kermit

B

14

12

Redbud Trail

400 m

0.2 miles

Lake
Austin

Tom Miller Dam

Red Bud
Isle

A

N

For reviews see	
● Top Sights	p106
◉ Sights	p112
✕ Eating	p113
● Drinking	p114
● Shopping	p116

1

2

3

4

10th St
W 9th St
W 8th St
Puett St
W 7th St
Wayside Dr
Norwalk Lo

Meriden La
Deep Eddy Ave
Hearn St

Upson St

✕7

◉13 Foster Ave

Lake Austin Blvd

Deep Eddy Pool
◉3

Eilers Park

Veterans Park

Mopac Expwy

E

◉15

◉1 Lady Bird Lake

Zilker Park

See Around
Dripping Springs Inset
(8mi)

D

Colorado River

BLUFFINGTON

Stratford Dr

Vance La

Yale St

Riley Rd

Hatley Dr

C

Stratford Dr

Ashworth Dr

ROLLINGWOOD

Ridgewood Rd

Around Dripping Springs

Colorado River

71

Burton Creek

Main Map
(12mi)

✕6

290

1826

Lake
Travis

Hamilton Pool
Preserve
◉2

Hamilton Pool Rd

12

Fitzhugh Rd

◉8

◉9

290

5 ✕

Dripping
Springs

150

◉11

12

B

3238

McGregor La

◉10

Onion Creek

290

0   10 km
0   5 miles

A

5

6

7

8

Sights

Lady Bird Lake
CANOEING

 1 Map p110, E8

Named after former first lady 'Lady Bird' Johnson, Lady Bird Lake looks like a river. And no wonder: it's actually a dammed-off section of the Colorado River that divides Austin into north and south. Get on the water at the rowing dock, which rents kayaks, canoes and stand-up paddle boards from $10 to $20 per hour Monday to Thursday, with higher prices on weekends and during major events. (☑512-459-0999; www.rowingdock.com; 2418 Stratford Dr; ⏰9am-6pm)

Hamilton Pool Preserve
WATERFALL

 2 Map p110, A7

How gorgeous is the pool beneath Hamilton Creek, which spills over limestone outcroppings just upstream from the Pedernales River? Let's just

---

> ### Understand
>
> ### A Drip by any other Name
>
> Dripping Springs is juggling two nicknames these days, drawing road trippers as the 'Gateway to the Hill Country' and impressing brides and grooms as the 'Wedding Capital of Texas.' And some locals have dubbed the place 'West of Weird,' a nod to folks keepin' it weird in Austin.

---

say reservations are needed to visit this lush box canyon and waterfall-fed swimming hole from late spring through early fall. The special spot sits within a 30,428-acre preserve, which is also home to the endangered gold-cheeked warbler, a striking yellow-crowned bird.

The preserve can also fill up on winter weekends, before the spring and summer busy season, so get there early if the weather is looking nice. (☑512-264-2740; https://parks.traviscountytx.gov; 24300 Hamilton Pool Rd; per vehicle $15; ⏰9am-6pm; reservations required May-Sep; ℗)

Deep Eddy Pool
SWIMMING

3 Map p110, E7

With its vintage 1930s bathhouse built as part of the Works Progress Administration, Texas' oldest swimming pool is fed by cold springs and surrounded by cottonwood trees. There are separate areas for waders and lap swimmers. (☑512-974-1189; www.deepeddy.org; 401 Deep Eddy Ave; adult/child under 11yr/12-17yr $8/3/4; ⏰9am-7:30pm Mon-Fri, 9am-7pm Sat & Sun)

Mayfield House & Nature Preserve
PARK

4 Map p110, E2

Did somebody say peacocks? Kids will love gawking at these showy birds while exploring the riverside trails and grounds at this low-key park beside Lake Austin. The park is a nice

Pit BBQ at Salt Lick

companion to Mount Bonnell, just up the road, if you want to do a bit more hiking and exploring. It's a good place to let younger kids run a little bit wild. No pets. (☎512-974-6700; 3805 W 35th St; admission free; 🚼)

Eating

Salt Lick BARBECUE $$

5 🍴 Map p110, B8

It's worth the 20-mile drive out of town just to see the massive outdoor barbecue pits at this parklike place off Hwy 290. It's a bit of a tourist fave, but the crowd-filled experience still gets our nod. Hungry? Choose the family-style all-you-can-eat option (adult/child $25/9). Cash only and BYOB. (☎512-858-4959; www.saltlickbbq.com; 18300 FM 1826, Driftwood; mains $10-22; ⏰11am-10pm; 🚼)

Pieous PIZZA $

6 🍴 Map p110, B8

Holy moly, this is good pie. Opened just a few years ago, this wood-fired pizza joint has earned kudos left and right. The motto here is 'food is our religion,' which gives a nod to the name of the place and to their focus on using fresh and homemade ingredients. The beloved pastrami is cooked in a BBQ smoker out back. (☎512-394-7041; www.facebook.com/pieous;

12005 W Hwy 290; pizzas $10-15; ⊙11am-2pm & 4-9pm Tue-Fri, 11am-9pm Sat, to 8pm Sun)

Magnolia Cafe
TEX-MEX **$**

7 Map p110, E7

In Westlake, opposite Deep Eddy Cabaret, this casual, all-night cafe serves American and Tex-Mex standbys such as *migas,* enchiladas, pancakes and potato scrambles. It gets absurdly crowded on weekends. (☎512-478-8645; www.themagnoliacafe. com; 2304 Lake Austin Blvd; breakfast $5-9, mains $7-16; ⊙24hr)

Drinking

Jester King Brewery
MICROBREWERY

8 Map p110, B7

Jester King may be the perfect country brewery. In a rural setting with picnic tables, cornhole games, shady oaks and a barn-style brewery, the backdrop is mighty picturesque, especially as the sun goes down. The long beer menu, with a focus on sour brews, is fun to sample. Hours may vary seasonally. (www.jesterkingbrewery. com; 13187 Fitzhugh Rd; ⊙4-10pm Fri, noon-10pm Sat, noon-7pm Sun)

Understand
Hill Country Wineries

When most people think of Texas, they think of cowboys, cactus and Cadillacs – not grapes. But the Lone Star State is a major wine producer, and the Hill Country, with its robust Provence-like limestone and hot South African-style climate, has become the state's most productive wine-making region. Sitting a short drive west and south of Austin, the rolling hills of the Hill Country are home to more than 50 wineries, with the largest concentration of vineyards found around Fredericksburg, primarily along Hwy 290.

Most larger wineries are open daily for tastings and tours. Many also host special events, such as grape stompings and annual wine and food feasts. Smaller wineries are typically open during set hours on weekends, but by appointment on weekdays. Local visitor bureaus stock the handy Texas Hill Country Wineries Guide & Map, which summarizes the wineries and pinpoints their locations (or visit www.texaswinetrail.com).

You could leave the driving to someone else with **Fredericksburg Limo & Wine Tours** (☎830-992-0696; www.texaswinelimos.com; tours per person $109-149), which offers limo tours or more affordable shuttle van tours. For a list of tour operators, check www.wineroad290.com, which covers wineries along Hwy 290 and provides a map of their locations.

Treaty Oak Distilling

9 Map p110, B7

This destination distillery is the perfect host: fun, friendly and a master when it comes to cocktails. Sample their spirits in the tasting room then head to one of the bars for a fine mixed drink. You can supplement your sipping with snacks, a burger or a sandwich from the on-site **Ghost Hill Restaurant** (snacks $2 to $10, mains $6 to $7). (☏512-599-0335; www.treatyoakdistilling.com; 16604 Fitzhugh Rd; ⏱3-9pm Fri, noon-9pm Sat, noon-6pm Sun)

Hawk's Shadow Winery

WINERY

10 Map p110, A7

This family-run winery is the full package: Texas hospitality, sweet views of the Hill Country from the patio and small-batch reds infused with Texas terroir – and that means easy drinking. Budding geologists can step into the cellar for a look at fossils found in the limestone here. (☏512-587-9085; www.hawksshadow.com; 7500 McGregor Ln; tasting per person $10; ⏱noon-6pm Sat, by appointment Wed-Fri & Sun; 👶)

Twisted X Brewing Co

MICROBREWERY

11 Map p110, B8

Open a bit earlier than other local microbreweries, Twisted X is an easygoing spot for a post-work drink. Ingredients from Texas and Mexico keep things regional. Try the tasty

Top Tip

Outdoor Art Beside the Lake

To complement your climb up Mount Bonnell with eye-catching outdoor art, make your way post-hike to the Betty and Edward Marcus Sculpture Park at **Laguna Gloria** (3809 W 35th St; www.thecontemporaryaustin.org; $5), the West Austin branch of Contemporary Austin (p34). Perfect for strolling, the sculpture-dotted grounds sprawl across 14 lush and woodsy acres beside Lake Austin. The sculpture park is open 9am to 5pm Monday through Saturday and from 10am to 5pm Sunday. Free admission on Tuesdays.

Fuego, which will kick your palate with a touch of jalapeño sass. (☏512-829-5823; www.twistedxbrewing.com; 23455 W RR 150; ⏱11am-9pm Thu-Sat, noon-8pm Sun)

Hula Hut

BAR

12 Map p110, B1

The hula theme is so thorough that this restaurant feels like a chain, even though it's not. But the bar's sprawling deck that stretches out over Lake Austin makes it a popular hangout among Austin's nonslackers. (☏512-476-4852; 3825 Lake Austin Blvd; ⏱11am-10pm Mon-Thu, to 11pm Fri, 10:30am-11pm Sat, to 10pm Sun)

Understand

Scenic Drive: Wildflower Trails in the Hill Country

Thanks to former First Lady Claudia Taylor Johnson – around here everyone calls her Lady Bird – each spring the highways are lined with stunning wildflowers that stretch for miles, planted as part of her Highway Beautification Act.

You know spring has arrived in Texas when you see cars pulling up roadside and families climbing out to take the requisite picture of their kids surrounded by bluebonnets – Texas' state flower. From March to April in the Hill Country, orange Indian paintbrushes, deep-purple wine-cups and white-to-blue bluebonnets are at their peak.

If a visit to the Ladybird Johnson Wildflower Center (p62) in South Austin has you itching for more blooms, hit the road for the nearby Hill County. To see vast cultivated fields of color, there's **Wildseed Farms** (📞830-990-1393; www.wildseedfarms.com; 100 Legacy Dr; admission free; ⏰9:30am-5pm), which is 7 miles east of Fredericksburg on Hwy 290.

For a more do-it-yourself experience, check with the Texas Department of Transportation (TXDOT) **Wildflower Hotline** (📞800-452-9292) to find out what's blooming where. Taking Rte 16 and FM 1323, north from Fredericksburg and east to Willow City, is usually a good route. Then again you might just set to wandering – most back roads host their own shows daily. At visitor centers, look for the Texas Wildflowers pamphlet from Texas Highways magazine. It identifies Lone Star flowers and provides routes for scenic wildflower drives.

Deep Eddy Cabaret
BAR

13 Map p110, E7

This great little neighborhood bar is known for its excellent jukebox, loaded with almost a thousand tunes in all genres. Yep, it's a dive, but a top-rate one. (📞512-472-0961; 2315 Lake Austin Blvd; ⏰noon-2am)

Mozart's Coffee Roasters
COFFEE

14 Map p110, B1

Out on Lake Austin, you'll find a great waterfront view and a sinful dessert case. (📞512-477-2900; 3825 Lake Austin

Blvd; ⏰7am-midnight Mon-Thu, 7am-1am Fri, 8am-1am Sat, 8am-midnight Sun)

Shopping

Barton Creek Mall
MALL

15 Map p110, E8

This indoor mall in southwest Austin has your standard mall offerings. (📞512-327-7041; www.simon.com/mall/barton-creek-square; 2901 S Capital of Texas Hwy; ⏰10am-9pm Mon-Sat, 11am-7pm Sun)

Bluebonnets and Indian paintbrush wildflowers in the Hill Country

Top Sights
San Antonio: The Alamo

Getting There

🚗 **Car** Downtown San Antonio is bordered by I-35, I-10 and I-37, with concentric rings of highways around the center. I-35 connects Austin and San Antonio.

It would be a shame to visit Austin without making the trip San Antonio, home of the Alamo. Find out why the story of the Alamo can rouse a Texan's sense of state pride like few other things. For many, it's not so much a tourist attraction as a pilgrimage – you might notice some visitors getting downright dewy-eyed at the description of how a few hundred revolutionaries died defending the fort against thousands of Mexican troops.

The Building

The main chapel building is now known as the Shrine. From here you can set off for a free history talk in the Cavalry Courtyard, hearing one of many perspectives on the actual events – which are somewhat in dispute – or browse the museum in the Long Barrack, which served as a residence for the Spanish priests and later as a hospital for Mexican and Texan troops. There's also a 17-minute film, which not only gives you another perspective on the battle, but is an excellent place to escape the heat.

Walk the Alamo

If you're interested in walking the front perimeter of the old fort, which extends beyond the chapel, and learning more details about the battle and its participants, join the one-hour guided Battlefield Tour ($15 per person). A 33-stop audio tour ($7) is self-guided and takes about 45 minutes. (Visitors taking the guided tour are also given the audio tour, since the Battlefield Tour does not cover all 33 stops.)

A Series of Missions

The Alamo is the first (and most impressive) in a series of Spanish-constructed missions. With the destruction by war or disease of many East Texas missions, the Spanish quickly built four more missions south of the Alamo, now collectively known as the Mission Trail. Religious services are still held in these mission churches.

☎ 210-225-1391

www.thealamo.org

300 Alamo Plaza

admission free

⊙ 9am-5:30pm Sep-Feb, to 9pm Mar-Aug

☑ Top Tips

▶ Seeing the Alamo for the first time? Many people are surprised to see that it's in the middle of downtown San Antonio, surrounded by tacky tourist attractions. But even more startling is its diminutive size. The first thing many people say when they first see the Alamo is, 'Wow, it's a lot smaller than I thought it would be!'

✗ Take a Break

Founded in 1917, nearby **Schilo's German Delicatessen** (☎ 210-223-6692; www.schilos.com; 424 E Commerce St; mains breakfast $6-8, lunch & dinner $6-9; ⊙ 7am-8:30pm Mon-Sat) offers good-value breakfasts and lunches.

Top Sights
San Antonio: River Walk

Getting There

🚗 **Car** Street parking is hard to find. There are plenty of public parking lots downtown, including with most of the major hotels; the lots generally cost $3 per hour, or $5 to $10 for 24 hours.

A little slice of Europe in the heart of downtown San Antonio, the 15-mile River Walk is an essential part of the San Antonio experience. This is no ordinary riverfront, but a charming canal and pedestrian street that is the main artery at the heart of San Antonio's tourism efforts.

Background

In 1921 floods destroyed downtown San Antonio when water 10ft deep gushed through the center of the city from the overflowing San Antonio River. As a result, the Olmos Dam was constructed to handle overflow and route the extra water around the downtown area through a canal called the Oxbow.

In 1938 the Works Progress Administration (WPA) assumed control of the canal's fate, and executed a plan to develop a central business district of shops and restaurants along a cobbled walk. More than 1000 jobs were created during the construction of River Walk, and the project is one of the most beautiful results of the WPA effort.

Riverfront Activities

You can meander past landscaped hotel gardens and riverside cafes, and linger on the stone footbridges that stretch over the water. During summer it gets mighty crowded, but at peaceful times (and as you get away from downtown) it's a lovely place to stroll, especially during the holidays, when it's bedecked with twinkling lights.

Feeling athletic? Once out of downtown, cycling to San Antonio's missions or museums via the River Walk is also an option. Check with **B-Cycle** (☏210-281-0101; www.sanantonio.bcycle.com; day/monthly pass $10/18), San Antonio's bicycle-sharing scheme, for rental locations.

River Walk Extension

The River Walk used to be just a downtown thing, but a $358-million project completed in 2013 extended it to the north and south. As part of the 8-mile Mission Reach expansion, you can walk south to the King William District and beyond to the Spanish missions. The new 4-mile Museum Reach stretches north to the San Antonio Art Museum, the Pearl Brewery complex and Brackenridge Park.

www.thesanantonio
riverwalk.com

☑ **Top Tips**

▶ For the best River Walk overview, hop on a **Rio San Antonio river cruise** (☏210-244-5700; www.riosanantonio.com; 706 River Walk; tour $10, river taxi one way $10, 24hr pass from $12; ◷9am-9pm).

✕ **Take a Break**

Dining and drinking options abound along the River Walk. Cool off with a house-made Italian-style ice cream from **Justin's Ice Cream Company** (☏210-222-2707; 245 E Commerce St, River Walk; small/large serving $4/6; ◷11am-11pm) on the riverfront.

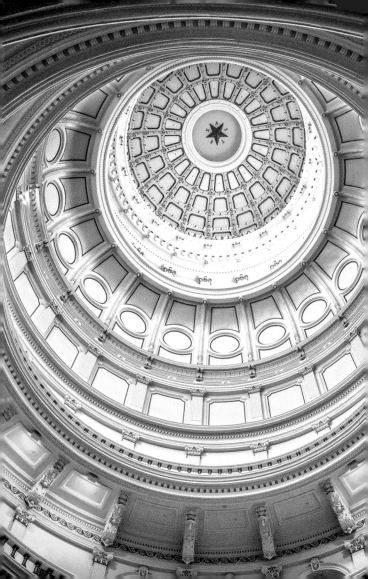

The Best of
Austin

Austin's Best Walks

Austin's Best...

Dome of the Texas State Capitol (p26)
SKY NOIR PHOTOGRAPHY BY BILL DICKINSON/GETTY IMAGES ©

Best Walks
Murals of South Austin

🏃 The Walk

Most people know about Austin's awesome food trucks, but the city is also home to an amazing collection of murals and wall art. Quirky, funny and sometimes poignant, the murals are unexpected treasures that bring a little joy to routine drives around the city. A few memorable images cluster in South Austin along S 1st St and Congress Ave.

Start Bouldin Creek Coffee House (p71)

Finish Amy's Ice Creams (p70)

Length 1.1 mile; 25 minutes

🍴 Take a Break

The open-air **Jo's Coffee** (p74) is a great spot for people-watching on S Congress Ave. Order your drink at the counter, plus a breakfast taco if it's early, and see who walks by. There will be a steady line of people queued to take of a photo in front of the *I Love You So Much* mural.

PETER TSAI PHOTOGRAPHY/ALAMY STOCK PHOTO

Jo's Coffee (p74)

❶ Bouldin Creek Coffee House

While you're waiting for your coffee at **Bouldin Creek Coffee House** (p71), take a moment to appreciate the wall art and feisty stickers plastered all over this busy place.

❷ Greetings from Austin

The bright **Greetings from Austin** (p68) mural on W Annie St doubles as an Instagram postcard. While you're here, someone will probably walk up to take a photo.

❸ Dazed & Confused

Stop just before W Monroe St for the **Dazed and Confused** (p69) mural depicting the 'Alright, Alright, Alright' scene with Matthew McConaughey in his role as Wooderson in Richard Linklater's classic movie *Dazed and Confused*, set in Austin.

4 Lady of Guadalupe

A bright and eye-catching portrait of the Lady of Guadalupe adorns the northern wall of the Tesoros Trading Company.

5 I Love You So Much

There will probably be a line waiting to take a selfie in front of the simple expression of affection spray-painted against the wall of Jo's Coffee, which reads:

I Love You So Much (p68). The mural is now so locally famous that it's been parodied on another wall or two around town. It was a declaration of affection, we hear, for a local hotelier from her girlfriend.

6 Austin Motel

The **Austin Motel** (1220 S Congress Ave) is known for its quirky rooms and vaguely phallic sign. There's usually a funny comment beneath it.

7 Amy's Ice Creams

The chalkboard list of ice creams at **Amy's Ice Creams** (p70) might be the most satisfying wall art on the walk – because it promises a delicious frozen treat.

Best Walks
Exploring Lady Bird Lake

🏃 The Walk

The city christened the trails encircling Lady Bird Lake the Ann & Roy Butler Hike-and-Bike Trail in 2011, named for an involved former mayor and his wife. A few years later, a full 10.1-mile trail around the lake was completed and several new features – from a lakeside boardwalk to artsy new restrooms – were introduced to the jogging and cycling masses. And we mean masses. The paths here experience 2.6 million visits per year.

Start Deep Eddy Pool

Finish Boardwalks

Length 3.5 miles; 1.5 hours

🍴 Take a Break

After your return to Deep Eddy Pool, make your way to the **Mean Eyed Cat** (p102), a welcoming neighborhood bar with an agreeable Johnny Cash obsession and a great patio.

❶ Deep Eddy Pool

If you picture an overgrown natural swimming hole when you hear the name **Deep Eddy Pool** (p112), think again. This Austin landmark, like Barton Springs Pool across the lake, is a man-made outdoor swimming pool, complete with a lifeguard and lap swimmers. It is unique in that it is fed by cold natural springs. Deep Eddy is the oldest swimming pool in the state.

❷ Johnson Creek Trailhead

A crossroads awaits at the Johnson Creek Trailhead across from Austin High School. You can walk cross the lake and head toward the Austin Nature & Science Center and other Zilker Park attractions on the south side of the lake, or continue east. Helpful signage at the trailhead provides the mileage for various loops around the lake via different bridges.

FLIPHOTO/SHUTTERSTOCK ©

Lady Bird Lake

❸ Texas Rowing Center

If the sight of all those folks paddling across the water inspires you to join them, stop by the lakeside **Texas Rowing Center** (www. texasrowingcenter. com), where you'll find kayaks, canoes and stand-up paddleboards for rent.

❹ Heron Creek Restrooms

The sleek new Heron Creek Restrooms blend form and functionality along the trail.

❺ Pfluger Pedestrian Bridge

The Pfluger Pedestrian Bridge, also open to cyclists, connects downtown to Butler Park on the south side of the lake. The bridge opened in 2001 as an alternative to the nearby Lamar Blvd Bridge, a narrow and heavily trafficked crossing point that was a dangerous route for walkers, joggers and cyclists.

❻ Austin-Chronicle Building

From the lawn of the Austin-Chronicle building near the Congress Ave Bridge, stake out a spot to watch the colony of Mexican free-tailed bats stream out along the river to feed, best seen April through November.

❼ Boardwalks

A series of new boardwalks stretch east for 1.1 miles along the river, offering stellar views of the downtown skyline.

Best
Food

The Austin food scene is innovative and downright delicious. Barbecue and Tex-Mex are mainstays, but fine-dining restaurants and world cuisines abound. Downtown eateries are a mixed bag, serving tourists, business folks, politicians, artists and night-owl clubbers. South Austin and East Austin have lots of interesting choices, including amazing food trucks. Around the UT campus prices drop – but often so does quality.

Food Trucks

From epicurean Airstreams to regular old taco trucks, food trailers are kind of a big deal in Austin, and wandering from one to another is a fun way to experience the local food scene. Because of their transient nature, we haven't listed any of these rolling restaurants, but since they travel in packs, we can tell you where they tend to congregate.

South Austin Trailer Park and Eatery This seems to be a rather settled trailer community, with a fence, an official name, a sign and picnic tables.

East Austin This area has its own little enclave, conveniently located right among all the bars on the corner of E 6th and Waller St.

Rainey St A cluster of food trucks is ready to serve the downtown hordes downing beers at nearby bars.

TANYA ISAEVA/SHUTTERSTOCK ©

Best Cheap Eats

Hopdoddy Burger Bar Join the line for gourmet burgers. (p71)

Veracruz All Natural Food truck that sells tacos so popular they hand you a buzzer. (p49)

Home Slice Stop by before or after South Congress fun for pizza. (p71)

Ramen Tatsu-ya Get your spicy ramen fix here. (p71)

Tacodeli Taco perfection made sublime by the spicy dona sauce. (p79)

Best Old Favourites

Guero's Taco Bar
Everybody loves Guero's
for the tacos, margaritas
and conviviality. (p73)

Chez Nous Fine French
fare off 6th St. (p37)

Texas Chili Parlor Load
up your chili with cheese
and sour cream. (p35)

Fonda San Miguel Old
Mexico dishes drawing
fans for 25 years. (p101)

Kerbey Lane Café
Great service, big menu,
delicious food – a winner.
(p99)

Best Evening Out

Uchiko Innovative sushi
and Japanese specialties
in warmly glossy digs.
(p98)

Dai Due Flavor-packed
fare from the butcher
next door and farms
nearby. (p52)

Barley Swine Seasonal
farm-to-table special-
ties and great cocktails.
(p100)

Wink Modern French and
Asian dishes are ready for
your date night. (p101)

Laundrette Lauded
newcomer serving
Mediterranean-inspired
meals. (p52)

Worth a Trip

They call it the
**Texas Barbecue
Trail** (www.texas
bbqtrails.com): 80
artery-clogging miles
of the best barbecuee
Texas has to offer,
stretching from Tay-
lor (36 miles north-
east of Austin) down
to Luling, passing
through Elgin and
Lockhart. Marketing
gimmick? Perhaps.
Do our stomachs
care? They do not. If
eating at 12 different
barbecue restaurants
is unfeasible, make
a beeline for brisket
in Lockhart, or, if
it's hot sausage you
crave, Elgin is your
best bet.

Best
Drinking

There are bejillions of bars in Austin. The legendary 6th St bar scene has spilled onto nearby thoroughfares, especially Red River St. Many 6th St places are shot bars aimed at college students and tourists. The Red River establishments retain a harder local edge. A few blocks south, Rainey St is also jumping, with old bungalows now home to watering holes. The coffee culture is strong.

MATT MUNRO/LONELY PLANET ©

6th Street Explained

Sixth St cuts across the city. In and around downtown, sections of the street have different nicknames when it comes to nightlife. Dirty 6th is the wild, bar-lined section stretching from Congress Ave east to I-35. East 6th refers to the burgeoning strip of restaurants and bars lining 6th St east of the I-35 in East Austin. West 6th, which is west of Congress Ave, has a few solid dive bars and live music venues. Also note that 6th St runs one-way, from east to west, between Hwy 1/MoPac Expy and the I-35.

Chicken Shit Bingo

We love Ginny's Little Longhorn Saloon (p101) any old time, but for a uniquely Austin outing, you've really got to experience the Sunday-night phenomenon known as chicken shit bingo. Beer-swilling patrons throw down their bets of $2 per square and wait to see what number the chicken 'chooses,' with the whole pot going to the winner. The chicken doesn't seem to mind, and most Sundays local favorite Dale Watson keeps everyone entertained while they wait for the results to drop.

☑ **Top Tip**

▶ Some of the best late-night bars don't serve food but you can recharge at food trucks permanently parked on the property, usually in the yard out back. Check the bar's website before heading out if you think you might get late-night munchies.

Coffee Culture

Austin's a laid-back kind of town, and there's no better way to cultivate your slacker vibe than hanging out, sipping coffee and watching everyone else doing the same. Most places offer light meals in addition to caffeinated treats.

Best Coffee

Bouldin Creek Coffee House Very representative of the South Austin scene, with a great vegetarian menu to boot. (p71)

Hideout Coffee House & Theatre Despite its downtown location, it has a near-campus vibe and damn fine brews. (p38)

Sa-Ten Coffee & Eats In an artists complex in East Austin, you can enjoy Japanese snacks with your latte. (p54)

Mozart's Coffee Roasters Out on Lake Austin you'll find a great waterfront view and a sinful dessert case. (p116)

Spider House North of campus, Spider House has a big, funky patio bedecked with all sorts of oddities. It's open late and also serves beer and wine. (p90)

Best for Craft Beer

Easy Tiger Laid-back beer garden between a creek and a bakery. (p37)

Craft Pride On Rainey St, only sells Texas beers. (p37)

ABGB Picnic tables, live music, great home brews and tasty pizza. (p73)

Scholz Garten Long-running downtown favorite with beers and barbecue. (p90)

Jester King Brewery In Dripping Springs, serving sour beers in a rustic setting. (p114)

Best Atmosphere

Driskill Hotel With taxidermy and leather couches, this clubby bar is prime for making deals. (p40)

Mean Eyed Cat The whole interior is an ode to Johnny Cash. (p102)

Hotel San Jose Hip style and fine drinks in a South Austin courtyard. (p73)

Whisler's If Austin has vampires, they surely lurk in this dark cocktail bar. (p53)

Garage Craft cocktails in a parking garage hideaway. (p37)

Best
Entertainment

When it comes to the performing arts, there is more to Austin than live music. The city is home to a thriving movie-going culture, an active local theater community and a strong comedy and improv scene. And college-football viewing at UT is no small affair, with average attendance per game topping 95,000.

RONALD MARTINEZ/GETTY IMAGES ©

Find a Perfomance

Heaps of information about the city's entertainment scene can be found in the *Austin Chronicle*, out on Thursdays, or on the *Austin American-Statesman's* 360 website (www.austin360.com). The latter has streamlined listings for concerts and nightlife. The *Chronicle's* night-by-night encyclopedia of listings often includes set times, plus music critics' picks and local gossip.

Live Music

These days most live-music bars and clubs have a mix of local and touring bands. On any given Friday night there are several hundred acts playing, and even on an off night (Monday and Tuesday are usually the slowest), you'll typically have your pick of more than two dozen performances. Often there are two or three bands per venue each night. Cover charges range from $5 for local bands to $15 or more for touring acts. Music shows often start late, with the headliner beginning anywhere from 9pm to midnight, though a few clubs offer music as early as 4pm. Doors almost always open half an hour to an hour before showtime. Showing up at the last minute or fashionably late may result in not getting in. If you want to start early, most places have a happy hour (4pm to 7pm).

Spectator Sports

The whole town turns burnt orange during University of Texas game weekends, especially during football season, when the fiercely loyal Longhorn fans are downright fanatical. (They're not flipping you off: it's probably just the two-fingered sign for 'Hook 'em Horns.') For tickets to any university-sponsored sporting event, contact the UT box office (p85).

Best Performance Venues

Cactus Cafe Listen to acoustic up close and personal at this intimate club on the UT campus. (p90)

Crowd-surfer at a South by Southwest (SXSW) performance

Frank Erwin Center
Known as 'The Drum' among UT students, this major venue for concerts and UT sports can hold up to 17,000 screaming fans. (p90)

Paramount Theatre
This old vaudevillian house dates from 1915. (p40)

Stubb's Bar-B-Q
Small indoor stage looks onto the main backyard concert venue, which rocks the Red River scene. Excellent acoustics. (p38)

Antone's
This key player in Austin's musical history has attracted the best of the blues and other popular local acts since 1975. All ages, all the time. (p38)

Best Music Festivals

South by Southwest (SXSW)
One of America's biggest and most varied music-industry gatherings. (www.sxsw.com; single festival $825-1325, combo pass $1150-1650; ☉mid-Mar)

Austin City Limits
Three-day autumn festival, held in Zilker Park. (www.aclfestival.com; 1-/3-day pass $100/250; ☉Oct)

Best Live-Music Venues in South Austin

Continental Club
Legendary 1950s-era lounge with a swingin' dancefloor. (p74)

Saxon Pub
Relaxed rock- and blues-oriented venue. (p75)

Emo's East
Standout venue hosting punk, rock and more. (p75)

Stubb's Bar-B-Q
Multiple stages and live music almost every night. (p38)

Best Dance Halls

Broken Spoke
Perhaps *the* authentic Texas honky-tonk in Austin. (p74)

Mercer Street Dance Hall
Live country music, two-stepping and ice-cold beer. (p109)

White Horse
Diverse and friendly honky-tonk. (p54)

Best
Shopping

Not many folks visit Austin just to shop, but there are enough homegrown indie shops with unique finds that it's worth setting aside a few hours to check out what's on offer.

PETER TSAI PHOTOGRAPHY/ALAMY STOCK PHOTO ©

Record Shops

Music is a huge industry here and you'll find heaps of it in Austin's record stores. Employees are usually fairly knowledgeable and will likely be in a band themselves. The best stores let you listen to just about anything before you buy, and will carry the bands you see around town.

Vintage Apparel & Furnishings

Vintage is a lifestyle, and the city's best hunting grounds for retro fashions and furnishings are South Austin and Guadalupe St near UT. For more vintage-fashion options, check out www.vintagearoundtownguide.com.

Best Arts & Antiques

Uncommon Objects Eclectic assortment of antiques on S Congress Ave. (p65)

Austin Art Garage Works from local artists with distinctive style. (p75)

Mexic-Arte Museum Fantastic Mexican crafts for sale in the gift shop. (p34)

Yard Dog Folk art with lots of personality is the draw at this South Congress gallery. (p76)

Tesoros Trading Co Colorful collection of folk art, much of it from Latin America. (pictured above left; p65)

Best Indie Shops

Allens Boots Cowboy boots by various makers fill the aisles. (p65)

☑ **Top Tip**

▸ For a list of art galleries and local happenings, visit www.artaustin.org.

Book People Inc Huge indie bookstore with author readings and great staff recommendations. (p95)

Waterloo Records Amazing vinyl selection and welcoming staff. (p95)

Big Top Candy Shop Old-fashioned candy, gummy bears and ice cream. What's not to love? (p65)

Toy Joy So many toys, so little time. (p41)

Best
Outdoor Activities

Austin has numerous places to play outside, including Zilker Park, Lady Bird Lake, and creekside parks and greenbelts.. You can get just about any information you might need from the City of Austin Parks & Recreation Department (www.austintexas.gov/department/parks-and-recreation). Check the website for everything from municipal golf courses to tennis complexes.

Cycling & Hiking

With 10 miles of trails looping around Lady Bird Lake, the Ann & Roy Butler Hike-and-Bike Trail & Boardwalk (p68) is a popular spot for exercise. The trail runs most of the way along the lake's northern side, which is the south edge of downtown Austin, and along the lake's southern side, buffering South Austin. The trail crosses the lake on several bridges, so it is easy to adjust your total distance. You can also hike or mountain bike for almost 8 miles along the Barton Creek Greenbelt (p79), which can be entered near Barton Springs Pool. If you visit the Lady Bird Johnson Wildflower Center, add time to ride or skate the great 3.2-mile Veloway track (p70) nearby. The track runs clockwise, and no walking or running is permitted.

Spring-Fed Pools & Swimming Holes

Austinites escape the heat at local swimming holes (often formed by cold springs). So pack your swimsuit if you're visiting the city in summer (although the pools are open year-round). You'll find popular spring-fed pools in Zilker Park, Dripping Springs and along the Barton Creek Greenbelt. No swimming is allowed in Lady Bird Lake, although you can paddle across it in watercraft.

Best Outdoor Activities

Barton Springs Pool Swim laps in a cold spring-fed pool. (p79)

Lady Bird Lake Rent a kayak and paddle on waters in view of downtown. (pictured above right; p112)

Ann & Roy Butler Hike-and-Bike Trail & Boardwalk Join the joggers on a loop around the lake. (p68)

Mount Bonnell Short climb leads to the highest point in the city and Lake Austin views. (p106)

Barton Creek Greenbelt Walk and bike this 8-mile greenway beside a lovely creek . (p79)

Hamilton Pool Preserve Swim in a lush box canyon pool beneath a waterfall. (p112)

Best
Weird Austin

For years, Austin's unofficial motto has been 'Keep Austin Weird.' Bumper stickers and T-shirts insist upon it, but are they succeeding? Check out www.keepaustinweird.com to find out what's odd right now.

LHB PHOTO/ALAMY STOCK PHOTO ©

History of Weird

When asked why he was a making a donation to The Lounge Show, a radio program that played unusual songs, back in 2002, Austin Community College librarian Red Wassenich said he wanted to 'Keep Austin Weird.' His wish soon became a rallying cry as the cheap and offbeat city became more corporate with all the new arrivals. Wassenich and his wife subsequently printed Keep Austin Weird bumper stickers, and he penned a book spotlighting the city's weirdest attractions. Today, ever-growing bedroom community Dripping Springs dubs itself West of Weird.

Best Weird Sights

Cathedral of Junk A climbable backyard sculpture that turns discarded items into art. (pictured above left; p70)

Museum of the Weird Animal deformities, shrunken heads and a live show! (p34)

Alamo Drafthouse Cinema Home to Master Pancake Theater and other offbeat events. (p38)

Ginny's Little Longhorn Saloon Chicken-shit bingo in this dive bar. (p101)

Christmas lights 37th St east of Lamar lights up in December.

Murals Eclectic artworks are scattered across the city.

Best Annual Events

Eeyore's Birthday Party An annual Festival where weirdness reigns supreme. (☏512-448-5160; www.eeyores.com; Pease Park, 1100 Kingsbury St; ⏰late Apr; 👫)

Austin Hot Sauce Festival Fiery sauces are feted in a hot month – August!

Bat Fest August festival honoring the city's Mexican free-tailed bats.

Best
For Free

It's easy to have fun on the cheap in this city, which is filled with starving artists, hardworking musicians and many students. Highlights include the nightly bat migration, murals and outdoor art, city parks and the state capitol complex.

KEN WOLTER/SHUTTERSTOCK ©

Best Free Sights

Austin Art Garage
Offbeat gallery that captures the spirit of Austin's art scene. (p75)

Elisabet Ney Museum
Former home of – and now gallery dedicated to – this important sculptor. (p88)

Texas State Capitol
This state capitol, built from sunset-red granite, is the largest in the US. Free tours too. (pictured above right; p26)

Mayfield House & Nature Preserve Look for the peacocks and stroll along the river. (p112)

Best Murals & Graffiti

Greetings from Austin
This colorful postcard will brighten any Instagram feed. (p68)

I Love You So Much
Couples pose before this simple declaration of affection. (p68)

Hi, How Are You Kurt Cobain wore a T-shirt adorned with this very frog. (p88)

Hope Outdoor Gallery
Artsy graffiti brightens building ruins for a good cause. (p98)

Dazed and Confused
Wooderson gets ready for the evening. Alright, alright, alright. (p69)

☑ **Top Tips**

▶ For more recommendations about free stuff to do in Austin, visit www.freesfuninaustin.com.

▶ Find free daily concerts and performances listed at www.do512.com/free.

Best
LGBTIQ Austin

ALEXANDER H. SCHULZ/GETTY IMAGES ©

With a thriving gay population – not to mention pretty mellow straight people – Austin is arguably the most gay-friendly city in Texas. Businesses and bars are typically welcoming across the city. The bar and club scene is centered in the Warehouse District downtown, particularly along W 4th St between Lavaca and Colorado Sts.

Resources

The **Austin Gay & Lesbian Chamber of Commerce** (3007 N Lamar Blvd; www.aglcc.org) sponsors the Pride Parade in August, as well as smaller events throughout the year. It also compiles a helpful online directory of gay-owned and -friendly businesses. For music and media-related events, visit www.Republiq.com. The **Austin Chronicle** (www.austinchronicle.com) runs the Gay Place, a gay event column. Radio station **97.5 Pride Radio** (www.975pride.iheart.com) programs music for LGBTIQ listeners and friends.

Around Texas

Although Texas is generally conservative, Austin and the larger cities have gay, lesbian, bisexual and transgender communities. But note that outside of Pride days and Austin in general, you won't see sexual preference being flaunted. In rural areas, displays of affection may draw negative attention from locals. We advise not trying it.

Best LGBT Bars

Oilcan Harry's Dance club for the boys. (p38)

Rain on 4th Dance club with weekly events. (217 W 4th St; www.rainon4th.com)

Highland Lounge
Get your sexy on with cocktails and dancing. There's a patio too. (404 Colorado St; www.highland lounge.com)

Cheer Up Charlies (900 Red River St; www. cheerupcharlies.com) Sip beer, wine and kombucha on the covered patio.

Best
Museums

SURSUM SCULPTURE AT ELIZABET NEY MUSEUM

BERNIE EPSTEIN/ALAMY STOCK PHOTO ©

Most of the city's museums cluster in two places: downtown and the University of Texas campus. The two art museums downtown are noted for their avant-garde and thoughtful temporary exhibits. In the UT area, museums tackle Texas history, art, natural science and written and photographic artifacts. Offbeat museums are scattered across town.

Best History Museums

Bob Bullock Texas State History Museum
A big museum spotlighting the state's big story. (p28)

Lyndon Baines Johnson (LBJ) Library & Museum Covers the background and social programs of the 36th president of the US. (p82)

Texas State Capitol
Guided and self-guided tours highlight historic and unique features. (p26)

Harry Ransom Humanities Research Center Spotlights written and photographic treasures. (p85)

George Washington Carver Museum Shares the history of Juneteenth and the stories of prominent Austin African American families. (p48)

Best Art Museums

Blanton Museum of Art
Check out the intriguing special exhibits. (p29)

Mexic-Arte Museum
Thought-provoking works from Mexican and Mexican American artists. (p34)

Contemporary Austin: Jones Center Up-to-the-minute art downtown, plus a statue garden in West Austin. (p34)

Best Unique Museums

Museum of the Weird
Offbeat and mysterious artifacts from around the world. (p34)

☑ **Top Tips**

▶ Admission to the Bob Bullock Texas State History Museum (p28) is free on the first Sunday of the month.

▶ The freestanding Capitol Visitors Center (p147) has several exhibits about the capitol building.

Elisabet Ney Museum
Statue-filled studio of one of Austin's great sculptors. (pictured above right; p88)

SouthPop Austin's cultural highlights covered here. (p70)

Best
For Kids

Austin is kid-friendly, thanks to the casual south-central Texas lifestyle. Zilker Park (p79) is always a good bet for outdoor fun, with loads of indoor and outdoor options.

INGA SPENCE/ALAMY STOCK PHOTO ©

Necessities

Dining It's more than fine to bring kids along to casual restaurants, which often have high chairs and children's menus.

Lodging Most motels and hotels offer rooms with two double beds, which are ideal for families. Some also have roll-away beds or cribs that can be brought into the room for an extra charge. Some hotels offer 'kids stay free' programs for children up to 18 years old. Most B&Bs do not allow children under 12 to stay.

Supplies Baby food, formula, soy and cow's milk, disposable diapers (nappies) and other necessities are widely available in drugstores and supermarkets. Breastfeeding in public is accepted when done discreetly. Many public toilets have a baby-changing table, and gender-neutral 'family' bathrooms may be available at airports, museums etc.

Best for Children

Zilker Zephyr Ride around Zilker Park on a miniature train. (pictured above; p79)

Austin Nature & Science Center Exhibits about Texas flora and fauna, plus trails In Zilker Park. (p61)

Barton Springs Pool Cool off in this ginormous natural pool with icy-cold water. (p79)

☑ **Top Tip**

▶ Mix your book-shopping with a children's storytime gathering on Saturdays at 11:30am at Book People Inc (p95).

Thinkery A new and much larger space for the former Austin Children's Museum. (p48)

Texas Memorial Museum Dinosaurs on the UT campus. (p88)

Mayfield House & Nature Preserve Peacocks and trails. (p112)

Survival Guide

Survival Guide

Before You Go

When to Go
Austin

°C/°F Temp
Rainfall inches/mm

40/104 —
— 8/200

30/86 —
— 6/150

20/68 —
— 4/100

10/50 —
— 2/50

0/32 —
— 0

J F M A M J J A S O N D

➡ **Spring (Mar–May)** Wildflowers and mild weather make this the perfect time of year to visit. Temperatures get hot in May.

➡ **Summer (Jun–Aug)** The weather is hot but bearable, and everything is still green for the most part.

➡ **Fall (Sep–Nov)** You won't see any fall foliage, but temperatures will have cooled by now.

➡ **Winter (Dec–Feb)** Temperatures can drop below 40° F, but warm and mild conditions are the norm. Snow is rare.

Book Your Stay

➡ There's no shortage of rooms, until major events come to town, such as SXSW, the Formula 1 Grand Prix, the Austin City Limits Festival and the Thanksgiving Day football game between UT and Texas A&M.

➡ At these peak times prices skyrocket and rooms are booked months in advance. At other times, choose accommodations as close to downtown as you can afford.

➡ Chains border I-35, and while they may not offer the best Austin experience, great deals can be found.

Useful Websites

Lonely Planet (www. lonelyplanet.com/usa/ austin/hotels) reviews of Lonely Planet's top choices.

Visit Austin (www. austintexas.org/visit/ stay/hotels/) City tourism website with overview of accommodation options plus lodging summaries.

Best Budget

Best Western Plus – Austin City (www.bestwestern.com) Complimentary breakfast is the bomb.

Star of Texas Inn (www.staroftexasinn.com;) No-fuss style – come and go like you own the place.

Firehouse Hostel (www.firehousehostel.com) Downtown hostel with a pub.

Drifter Jack's (www.drifterjackshostel.com) Murals and hospitality near UT.

HI-Austin (www.hiusa.org/austin) Cheerful place near Lady Bird Lake in South Austin.

Best Inns & Small Hotels

Heywood Hotel (www.heywoodhotel.com) Style and hospitality in East Austin.

Kimber Modern (www.kimbermodern.com) A posh and tranquil oasis near S Congress Ave.

Hill Country Casitas (www.hillcountrycasitas.com) Stone cottages on a terraced hillside.

Hotel Ella (www.hotelella.com) History and art near the University of Texas.

Best Boutique Hotels

Hotel Van Zandt (www.hotelvanzandt.com) Glossy, music-themed and over-looking the lake.

South Congress Hotel (www.southcongresshotel.com) Great patios and bars for people-watching.

Hotel San Jose (www.sanjosehotel.com) Stylish courtyard is the place to be.

Hotel St Cecilia (www.hotelsaintcecilia.com) As exclusive as you can get in Austin.

Lone Star Court (www.lonestarcourt.com) Cowboy cool with loads of amenities.

Arriving in Austin

Austin-Bergstrom International Airport

Opened in 1999, Austin-Bergstrom International Airport is about 10 miles southeast of downtown. It's served by Air Canada, Alaska Airlines, Allegiant, American, British Airways, Delta, Frontier, Jet-Blue, Southwest, United and Virgin America.

Ground Transportation

Lower level near baggage claim.

Taxi Between the airport and downtown costs $25 to $30.

Capital Metro Runs a limited-stop Airport Flyer (bus 100) service between the airport and downtown and the University of Texas for just $1.25 each way, with departures every 30 minutes. Check website for exact schedules. It takes at least 20 minutes to get downtown from the airport, and 35 minutes to reach the UT campus.

SuperShuttle (☎800-258-3826; www.supershuttle.com) Offers shared-van service from the airport to downtown hotels for about $14 one way, or a few dollars more to accommodations along N I-35 and near the Arboretum Mall.

Rental Cars Walk from the terminal to the rental car facility. All major rental car agencies are represented.

Shared Ride Companies that pick-up and drop-off passengers at the airport

include Fare (www.ride
fare.com), Fasten (www.
fasten.com) and the
non-profit Ride Austin
(www.rideaustin.com),
plus a few others. Uber
(www.uber.com) and Lyft
(www.lyft.com) recently
resumed operations in
the city.

Bus

Greyhound (☏512-458-4463; www.greyhound.
com; 916 E Koenig Lane)
Station is 5 miles north of
downtown. Capital Metro
bus 10-South First/Red
River (www.capmetro.
org) will deliver you from
the station to downtown.
Buses leave from here for
other major Texas cities
frequently.

Megabus (☏800-256-2757; www.megabus.com;
1500 San Jacinto Blvd) Pick-
up and drop-off stop at
1500 San Jacinto Blvd on
the northeast corner of
the state capitol grounds.

Train

Amtrak (☏512-476-5684;
www.amtrak.com; 250 N
Lamar Blvd) The downtown
station is served by
the Texas Eagle, which
extends from Chicago to

Los Angeles. There's free
parking and an enclosed
waiting area but no staff.
Fares vary wildly.

Getting Around

Bicycle

A grand bicycle tour
of greater Austin isn't
feasible, due to interstate
highways and the like, but
cycling around downtown,
South Congress and the
UT campus is totally do-
able. There are also miles
of recreational paths
around the city that are
ideal for cruisin'. Check
https://austintexas.gov/
bicycle for a route map.
You'll also find routes and
maps at www.bicycleaus
tin.info.

The city also offers bike
sharing, with more than
40 **Austin B-cycle** (www.
austin.bcycle.com) stations
scattered around the city.

Say what you will about
Lance Armstrong, you can
still count on him to find
you a pretty good bike.
Located right downtown,
**Mellow Johnny's Bike
Shop** (☏512-473-0222;
www.mellowjohnnys.com; 400
Nueces St; day use $20-50;

⊙7am-7pm Mon-Fri, 7am-6pm
Sat, 8am-5pm Sun) is co-
owned by the disgraced
seven-time Tour de France
winner. It rents high-
performance bikes as well
as commuter bikes, and
offers free guided bike
rides (check the website
for a schedule).

Looking for something
more casual? The cool
thing about **Bicycle Sport
Shop** (☏512-477-3472; www.
bicyclesportshop.com; 517 S
Lamar Blvd; per 2hr from $16;
⊙10am-7pm Mon-Fri, 9am-
6pm Sat, 11am-5pm Sun) is its
proximity to Zilker Park,
Barton Springs and the
Lady Bird Lake bike paths,
all of which are within a
few blocks. Rentals range
from $16 for a two-hour
cruise on a standard bike
to $60 for a full day on a
top-end full-suspension
model. On weekends and
holidays, advance reservations are advised.

Car & Motorcycle

Getting around Austin
is easy enough, but the
main consideration for
drivers – other than rush-
hour gridlock and what
people from other towns
consider crazy drivers –
is where to leave your car
when you're not in it.

Downtown, the best
deal is at the **Capitol**

Visitors Parking Garage

(201 San Jacinto Blvd). It's free for the first two hours, and only $1 per half-hour after that, maxing out at $12. Other downtown garages and lots are fairly abundant. They usually charge $2 to $3 per hour, with a daily maximum of $10 to $18.

Other downtown garages and parking lots typically charge a flat fee of around $7 to $10 or so after dark. People also park for free under I-35 at the east end of 6th St, but you can't depend on it being available (or legal).

Parking meters downtown cost $1.20 per hour. Outside of downtown they usually run about $1 per hour, although rates may vary on the UT campus or within the State Capitol Complex. Gone are the days of free downtown street parking on nights and weekends. However, to discourage drunk driving after partying downtown, the city implemented the Get Home Safe Program. You can now prepay at meters that have yellow Next Day buttons. If you forget to prepay, you may have the ticket waived if you complete and email a waiver form stating you took a safe ride home.

Your car will not be towed – unless you park on 6th St between Red River and Brazos Sts. Visit www.austintexas.gov/gethomesafe for more overnight parking and safe travel options.

Elsewhere around Austin, you can find free on-street parking, but pay careful attention to posted permit parking and time limits.

Day or night, finding a spot around the UT campus can take a while. Free visitor parking is available outside the LBJ Library in Lot 38, but from there it's a long, hot walk across campus to the UT Tower and other sights. Parking spots on Guadalupe St are both timed and metered. Otherwise, your best bet is to search for free parking in the residential streets west of Guadalupe St.

Public Transportation

Austin's handy public-transit system is run by **Capital Metro** (CapMetro; ☎512-474-1200, transit store 512-389-7454; www.capmetro.org; transit store 209 W 9th St; ⏱transit store 7:30am-5:30pm Mon-Fri). Call for directions to anywhere or stop into the downtown Capital Metro Transit Store for information. Regular city buses – not including the more expensive express routes – cost $1.25. Children under six years of age are free. There are bicycle racks (where you can hitch your bike for free) on the front of almost all CapMetro buses, including more than a dozen UT shuttle routes.

Ride Share

For ride sharing, try Fare (www.ridefare.com), Fasten (www.fasten.com) or the non-profit Ride Austin (www.rideaustin.com). Uber (www.uber/com) and Lyft (www.lyft.com) recently resumed service in the city.

Taxi

You'll usually need to call for a cab instead of just flagging one down on the street, except at the airport, at major hotels, around the state capitol and at major entertainment areas. The flag drops at $2.50, then it's $2.40 for each additional mile. Larger companies include **Yellow Cab** (☎512-452-9999) and **Austin Cab** (☎512-478-2222) .

Human-powered bicycle taxis, or pedicabs, are available downtown on 6th St and around the Warehouse District, usually from about 9pm until after 2am from Wednesday to Saturday evenings. The drivers, who are typically young students or musicians, work entirely for tips, so please be generous.

Essential Information

Business Hours

Opening hours are included in reviews; below are generalities. Sight and activity hours vary throughout the year and may decrease during the shoulder and low seasons.

Banks 9am to 5pm Monday to Friday

Restaurants 11am to 2pm and 5pm to 10pm, often without breaks.

Cafes 7am to 8pm

Night clubs 8pm to 2am

Shops 9am to 6pm Monday to Saturday, 11am to 6pm Sunday

Discount Cards

AAA Membership in the American Automobile Association provides access to hotel room discounts, and some reduced admission as well as roadside assistance.

Seniors If you are over the age of 65, discount rates on hotel rooms and attractions may be available. Having an American Association of Retired Persons (AARP) card is not usually required.

Students An ISIC or official school ID card often gets you discounts on admission to museums and other attractions.

Electricity

120V/60Hz

Money

➡ Credit cards are widely accepted, and they are generally required for reservations and car rentals.

➡ ATMs accepting most network and credit cards are easily found, except in the most popular nightlife areas, where privately owned ATMs (look for them inside convenience stores or often right on the street) charge exorbitant transaction fees.

➡ Bank of America exchanges foreign currency and traveler's checks. There is an exchange service at the airport, too.

Public Holidays

Banks, schools, and government offices (including post offices) are closed on major holidays. Public holidays that fall on a weekend are often observed on the following Monday.

New Year's Day January 1

Confederate Heroes' Day January 19

Martin Luther King Jr Day Third Monday in January

President's Day Third Monday in February

Texas Independence Day March 2

Easter Sunday March/April

Memorial Day Last Monday in May

Independence Day July 4

Labor Day First Monday in September

Columbus Day Second Monday in October

Veterans Day November 11

Thanksgiving Fourth Thursday in November

Christmas Day December 25

Safe Travel

➡ Some folks may tell you that anywhere east of I-35 is dangerous. While there is some truth to that, overt or covert racism – this is a predominantly African American and Latino part of town – may exaggerate claims of danger.

➡ One major complaint is drunken college students letting it all hang out on 6th St. It's a party atmosphere, and if you're drunkenly counting your cash and appraising your jewelry in an alley at 2am, you're as likely to encounter interest here as anywhere else.

➡ Transients and panhandlers congregate downtown near Congress Ave, especially from 4th through 7th Sts. Keep your wits about you when returning to your car at night, or hail a taxi (or a pedicab).

➡ Austin natives claim they live in the allergy capital of America, and at any time of year residents and visitors are likely to sneeze and wheeze. If you're at all susceptible, especially to pollen or mold, bring proper medication.

Tourist Information

The bulletin boards found outside coffeehouses, cafes and grocery stores are a great source of news about local events, special activities and classified ads.

Austin Visitor Information Center (☎512-478-0098; www.austintexas.org; 602 E 4th St; ◷9am-5pm Mon-Sat, from 10am Sun) Maps, brochures and gift shop downtown.

Capitol Visitors Center (CVC; ☎512-305-8400; www.tspb.texas.gov/prop/tcvc/cvc/cvc.html; 112 E 11th St; ◷9am-5pm Mon-Sat, noon-5pm Sun) Stop here for self-guided tour maps of the capitol and tourist information about Austin and the state.

Travelers with Disabilities

Download Lonely Planet's free Accessible Travel guide from http://lptravel.to/AccessibleTravel.

Public Spaces

Guide dogs May legally be brought into restaurants, hotels and other businesses.

Lodging Most hotels and motels have rooms set aside for disabled guests.

Public buildings Hotels, restaurants, theaters, museums etc are required by the Americans with Disabilities Act (ADA) to be wheelchair accessible and have accessible restroom facilities.

Road crossings Street crossings are dangerous in Austin, with dozens of fatalities over the years. City Council has been considering audible crossing signals, but they are not yet in use.

Resources

Access-able Travel Source (www.access-able.com) Travel information and links.

Mobility International USA (www.miusa.org) Advises disabled travelers.

Wheelchair Getaways (www.accessible-mini vans.com/texas-austin. htm) Van rental.

Visas

➡ Visa rules change frequently and travelers should always double-check current requirements at the Department of State (http://travel. state.gov/visa), where downloadable forms are available.

➡ Currently, under the US Visa Waiver Program (VWP), visas are not required for citizens of 38 countries, including the United Kingdom, Australia, New Zealand, EU countries, South Korea and Japan.

➡ Citizens of (VWP) countries must request travel authorization from Electronic System for Travel Authorization (ESTA; https://esta.cbp. dhs.gov) at least 72 hours in advance. Visitors not eligible for the program will require a B-2 tourism visa in advance of their arrival.

➡ Visa waiver is good for 90 days, no extensions. You must have an e-Passport with electronic chip. VWP visitors must register only with the ESTA at least 72 hours before their trip begins. Once approved, ESTA registration is valid for up to two years. If you don't meet any of these requirements, even if your passport is from one of the listed countries, you'll need a visa to enter the USA. Note that though not a part of the VWP, citizens from Canada do not require a visa for 90-day stays.

➡ All foreign visitors who need to obtain a temporary visitor visa (B-2) must do so from a US consulate or embassy abroad. Consult that embassy's website for forms and procedures, which vary by country.

Behind the Scenes

Send Us Your Feedback

We love to hear from travelers – your comments help make our books better. We read every word, and we guarantee that your feedback goes straight to the authors. Visit **lonelyplanet.com/contact** to submit your updates and suggestions.

Note: We may edit, reproduce and incorporate your comments in Lonely Planet products such as guidebooks, websites and digital products, so let us know if you don't want your comments reproduced or your name acknowledged. For a copy of our privacy policy visit lonelyplanet.com/privacy.

Amy's Thanks

Thank you for your Austin recommendations and hospitality: Chris McCray, Doug Kilday, Ken Wiles and family, John Apperson and Amanda Bachman. For fine party throwing and fierce BBQ opinions, thanks to the Austin W&L crew and their families: Jenny Stratton, Anna Salas, Kelly Rogers, Lucy Anderson, Bitsy and David Young, Chris Casey and John Pipkin. Thank you Paul and Crystal Sadler for the San Antonio tips. Finally, thanks to Alex Howard for entrusting me with this awesome assignment.

Acknowledgements

Cover photograph: Texas State Capitol, Kav Dadfar/4Corners ©
Contents photograph (pp4-5): Texas State Capitol, amadeustx/Shutterstock ©

This Book

This 1st edition of Lonely Planet's *Pocket Austin* guidebook was researched and written by Amy C Balfour and Stephen Lioy. This guidebook was produced by the following:

Destination Editor
Alexander Howard

Product Editor
Joel Cotterell

Senior Cartographer
Alison Lyall

Book Designer
Virginia Moreno

Assisting Editors James Bainbridge, Melanie Dankel, Bruce Evans, Carly Hall, Ali Lemer, Simon Williamson

Cover Researcher
Marika Mercer

Thanks to Kate Mathews, Martine Power, Victoria Smith, Tony Wheeler

Index

See also separate subindexes for:
Eating p152
Drinking p152
Entertainment p153
Shopping p153

Sights 000
Map Pages **000**

Sights **p000**
Map Pages **p000**

Our Writers

Amy C Balfour

Amy practiced law in Virginia before moving to Los Angeles to try to break in as a screenwriter. After a stint as a writer's assistant on *Law & Order,* she jumped into freelance writing, focusing on travel, food and the outdoors. Amy has hiked, biked and paddled across the United States. She recently crisscrossed Texas in search of the region's best barbecue and outdoor attractions. Books authored or coauthored include *USA, Eastern US, New Orleans, Florida & the South's Best Trips, New England's Best Trips, Arizona, Hawaii, Los Angeles Encounter* and *California.* Her stories have appeared in *Backpacker, Sierra, Southern Living* and *Women's Health.*

Contributing Writer

Stephen Lioy contributed to the Survival Guide chapter

Published by Lonely Planet Global Limited
CRN 554153
1st edition – Feb 2018
ISBN 978 1 78657 716 0
© Lonely Planet 2018 Photographs © as indicated 2018
10 9 8 7 6 5 4 3 2 1
Printed in Malaysia